Report on England

November, 1940

BY

RALPH INGERSOLL

Simon and Schuster · New York · 1940

MANUFACTURED IN THE UNITED STATES OF AMERICA
AMERICAN BOOK–STRATFORD PRESS, INC., NEW YORK, N. Y.

PUBLISHERS' FOREWORD

Ralph Ingersoll gathered the material for this book and wrote it all down in a space of less than five weeks. We have had it printed and published in a space of less than three weeks. Under such circumstances, both the author and the publisher suffer from certain handicaps, but with a story like this to tell, speed is not only important; the urgency of the story is increased by the pressure under which it has appeared. Ralph Ingersoll went to England in October, a month after Hitler's air Blitzkrieg on the British Isles had passed its peak. He stayed there barely two weeks, spending all his time in and near London. He wrote nothing while he was there, but immediately upon his return to America he described what he had seen in a series of articles that appeared in his own paper, PM, and in other newspapers throughout the country. This book reproduces those articles. There has been some change of sequence in order to integrate the individual articles into a full-length book—the first of its kind. It is the work of an American who flew across the Atlantic to see with his own eyes Britain at war and who flew back to the United States to tell his story.

The Publishers

TABLE OF CONTENTS

TOTAL WAR, TOTAL DE-FENSE, TOTAL CRISIS

THE STRANGEST sensation I had on getting back from England came from looking casually through the pages of *Vogue* magazine. Here in its smooth, white-coated pages was the written and pictured record of hundreds and hundreds of thousands of lives obviously enormously concerned with matters so trivial as to seem to me utterly and literally fantastic. It was as if I had arrived on Mars to find a nation of grown-up men and women whose lives were wholly dedicated to the cultivation and worship of the petunia.

Ernest Hemingway has written a very great book called *For Whom the Bell Tolls* and not the least of its morals is that a whole lifetime can be lived in three days. I did not live a lifetime in two weeks in London. But I think I spent a good many years in those fourteen days. Somehow it isn't only London that you feel when you're there but the whole continent of Europe, blacked out and grim. You feel not just the few million people immediately around you but also the scores and hundreds of millions of people that stretch from where you stand in the dark all the way around the world to the East, until in your imagination you come again upon the green of the Hawaiian Islands and know that beyond there are the Golden Gate and America again. For to the East there are the Germans who are starving for the privilege of killing you and, beyond them, the Poles and the Czechs whose days and nights must never seem to end and then the land where twenty years ago there was a people's revolution and where now six million men may not plow their fields or build their houses or sew together their clothes but must drill and drill and practice the art of killing with no profit to their own or anyone else's society because, like the rest of the world, they are frightened. And beyond the Russians there are the bravest and most determined people in all the world—the Chinese, whose courage and determination and success make all the other anti-Fascists in the world look like sissies in comparison—not even the combat pilots of the RAF excepted. And then you come to the coast that the Japanese hold, where they install their puppet governments and have the trains blown up. And all the way around in this great arc there are first millions and then tens of millions and then scores of millions and then hundreds of millions of people. Who in all those tens and scores and hundreds of millions could sit and look at *Vogue* magazine with me and understand it, no matter how well I translated? Some will have a *Vogue* magazine in their memories but the memories would be too unreal to interest them. It would be as boring for them to talk for more than a few minutes about their memories of a world that included *Vogue* as it would be for you to reminisce with a childhood friend about what kind of ice cream was served at the party you went to when you were ten.

It wasn't until I sat and looked through the pages of *Vogue* that I knew how much older I was than when I had left New York a month before.

Vogue magazine is made by cutting down trees in the forests of Canada and floating them to a paper mill.

Vogue magazine is made by mining the coal to stoke the boilers of the locomotives that pull the cars whose wheels are made of iron from the Mesabi Range—and all to bring the paper from the paper mill to Greenwich, Connecticut. *Vogue* magazine is made of 259,000 members of Sidney Hillman's garment union—and of their fighting for two generations for the right to bargain collectively with their employers. And all this effort to reproduce half-tone cuts of costume jewelry.

Vogue magazine is the photoelectric engraving process and a system of public education which includes courses in fashion designing and photography. *Vogue* magazine is the advertising-agency structure which has made so many millionaries and used to lay the keels for so many yachts. *Vogue* magazine is a cable under the Atlantic to carry the news that men will be allowed to look at women's knees on the street next year. *Vogue* magazine is an avenue of shops down which an industry parades.

Vogue magazine is peace and the right to live in childish fantasies and play house and dress up—all your life.

The reason that *Vogue* magazine made such an impression on me, I think, is that I saw it in London too— in a girl in a mink coat with orchids on it and her painted toenails showing through the silk stockings that can't be sold after December 1, and the cleft in the toe of her shoe which was so obviously inconvenient when she stepped over the rubble at the edge of the bomb crater. She was *Vogue* magazine in capsule form—distilled and concentrated like vitamins in a cod-liver-oil pill. And as you saw her there stepping daintily through the rubble you knew that *Vogue* magazine was through. She was its last outpost—eastbound between New York and all around the world to Hawaii where she would be lying on the beach in swimming pants and a brassière, a few miles from where they were building the Pearl Harbor naval base.

When she stepped down the muddy streets in Paris in 1789 the industrial revolution had begun and the political revolutions were right around the corner. And wise men knew that she was through then. But they could have told the end was a long way off because the people resented her, so they first whispered and then shouted at her and finally they cut off her head at the guillotine. She must have been very powerful to be so resented. In London when I saw her stepping through the rubble there were neither whispers nor catcalls and nobody proposed to guillotine her. Because she was so really through. No one was interested. As long as she could get someone to trap her minks, cultivate her orchids, and bring her silk from Japan—more power to her. She was a lot more satisfying to look at than a bombed building. But the minks came from Russia, the silk from Japan, and the man who grew the orchids was too old to fight and would soon be too old to grow orchids.

The sense that I brought back with me from England was the understanding which my heart had long felt and which I had known with my head but never really understood: that the world in which I had grown up was really over. Over, here as well as there. For the world I had grown up in was and is one with the rest of the world, however deceiving is the illusion of distance that the oceans give us. And the world, from England east through Germany and Russia and China and Japan all the way around back to our own coast, is no longer the world I had grown up in.

It is unrecognizably changed and irretrievably lost. And what we the American people have to realize is that *Vogue* magazine, which only a few years ago was very real, is now only a temporary illusion. A year, two years, five years, ten. Absolutely, certainly, no more. What lost France and almost lost England was that the Frenchmen and the Englishmen did not realize when they flew in the bomber without bombs to Munich that the world they'd grown up in was already no more than a passing temporary illusion.

No important leader but Roosevelt has really seen that in this country—clearly and for a decade. But thank God he has. Thank God that with all its mistakes the New Deal has done as much as it has to face the reality of a changed world and to try to find for ourselves a way in which we can live in it and still keep the right to wrestle with our own social problems and not have solutions imposed upon us by self-appointed "saviors." The Russians had a leader who saw it and his solution has been to sacrifice this generation's freedom for a promise to the next, not knowing whether he can ever fulfill that promise. The Germans had a leader who understood it better than the Russians. He understood it with the cunning of a rat. He has grown so fat in his understanding, and his teeth are so long and hard and sharp, that unless our understanding matches his—our understanding of the totality of the crisis of civilization—he will keep on growing fatter until it will take a generation of rat killers to de-Hitlerize the world, until we can get back to the peaceful process of learning how to live with the machines we have created to make life livable.

More power to *Vogue* magazine and long may it publish. But don't let it fool you. The world which created it is no more. The world in which your children will grow up you must make for them now, with your own blood and sweat and tears and—Churchill should have added, with your laughter.

REPORT ON ENGLAND

HITLER HAD LONDON
ONCE

I HAVE JUST returned from London, flying through the Nazi aerial blockade to Lisbon, thence to New York by Clipper. I was in England fourteen days. For ten of them I was in London, spending the nights going from shelter to shelter and the days talking to government officials and cabinet ministers and going over the city and its defenses on foot and by car. I was given complete freedom of action and used it as best I knew how.

Four days I spent with the RAF visiting the commanding officers of the three important commands—the fighter, the bomber, and the coastal—talking with literally scores of young pilots who have fought through the aerial *blitz*, their squadron leaders, their group commanders, their wing commanders. I spent a day at the experimental station where new planes and captured planes are tried out and tested. I spent a morning looking down on Germany through the RAF's magnifying lens, at aerial photographs of bombed military objectives, taken 30,000 feet in the air. I visited the field from which the most mysterious and terrifying of Britain's secret weapons is launched, the dread night fighter that is striking down two to five enemy bombers a night from 20,000 feet in

the air, at 300 miles an hour, in the pitch-black dark.
I saw the machines take off with no lights to guide them.

I spent forty continuous minutes looking through the
windshield sights of British pilots, plastering Nazi planes
with machine-gun fire in actual combat in the air—I was
seeing the film exposed in the camera guns that synchronize with the machine guns of the British fighters,
and so make a permanent documentary record of every
shot fired in actual combat.

I was going over the battlefield of the Battle of London. I was meeting the pilots who fought in it, the officers who directed them, civilians and civilian officials—
policemen, firemen, ARP wardens, aircraft spotters—
and the journalists who were there and saw and felt it
all. I have talked with literally hundreds of men and
women who were and are part of it.

I am writing the story of my trip—of what I saw and
heard with my own eyes and ears—as fast as I can (since
I only took notes when I was in the field). But the biggest news that I've come back with is this: that in the
month of September, between Saturday, September 7,
and Sunday, September 15, Hitler took London and
didn't know it. Goering's *Luftwaffe* took it for him in an
almost continuous succession of mass daylight raids
which for all practical purposes had the city on fire, its
transportation disrupted, its streets full of glass and
bricks, its water system practically out, its unprepared
civilian population holding on despite almost continuous and uninterrupted terror, with only their almost unbelievable courage and faith in themselves to maintain
them—because all through that week no one who was
there had any reason whatever to suppose that they and
their city would not be bombed and burned out of
existence.

On the ninth day of this ordeal—during the afternoon
of Sunday, the fifteenth of September, Adolf Hitler met

his first defeat in eight years. Only 185 of the *Luftwaffe's* planes were claimed by the British, but it is certain that well over 200 were destroyed. No one knew it at the time, but the continuous terror was over. A majority of responsible British officers who fought through this battle believe that if Hitler and Goering had had the courage and the resources to lose 200 planes a day for the next five days, nothing could have saved London.

Because those were all the German planes the RAF could shoot down a day and the RAF was weakening then. And, the losses aside, the Germans were winning—damaging precious industrial plants, disrupting communications, setting fire to their enemy's capital city.

For the four days preceding the fifteenth, photographs of the German side of the Channel had shown Hitler concentrating ships for the invasion—cargo boats, barges, scows, everything that floats, moving them steadily and by the thousands down the coast. The officers who took and studied them do not believe the invasion attempt was ever launched. They believe the *Luftwaffe's* losses on that Sunday afternoon stopped it when it was in its earliest phase.

The battle that was fought in the air over London between September 7 and 15 may go down in history as a battle as important as Waterloo or Gettysburg. Like Gettysburg, it may be recorded as a battle that the loser had won and didn't know it.

The *Luftwaffe* over England has never been the same since. Its morale in combat is definitely broken, and the RAF has been gaining in strength each week.

After the fifteenth the *Luftwaffe* did not come back en masse by daylight until the twenty-sixth and twenty-seventh of September. On each of those days they actually lost over a hundred planes—the official reports are 98 on the twenty-sixth and 133 on the twenty-seventh. It's been seven weeks now since then. The RAF is much stronger in men, machines, organization, and reserves. There are no more unprepared civilians in London. Every man, woman, and child who lived through September is a veteran who knows how to take care of himself, as the Madrileños learned how to take care of themselves during the years of bombing of Madrid. Today the *Luftwaffe* comes over London by day only in pursuit ships which can carry only one or two small bombs and cannot hit anything accurately except in isolated hit-and-run dives. Bombers can come only by night and can bomb with even a semblance of accuracy only once a month—and then only if they are lucky enough to catch clear weather when the moon is full and they can see its reflection in surface water to steer by. That is how they managed the massacre at Coventry. Their wireless-directed bombs, which I will explain presently, are accurate only along a path three miles wide.

The aerial attack on England began in the month of August. For ten days the *Luftwaffe* felt out the coastal defenses. It sparred with the RAF over Dover, as a contender spars with the champion in the first round of a fight, measuring his reach, limbering his muscles. By the tenth, the air over Dover was full of Germans, and correspondents were sending back word that the *blitz* was on. By the thirteenth the fighting was above the Thames estuary.

It was on the fourteenth that the Germans tried their parachute trick. The German short wave announced that *saboteurs* were being landed. Empty chutes were found all over England with their harnesses loosened to suggest that the occupants had just left. It was heavy-handed, orthodox *blitz* terror tactics and the British did not fall for it. But everyone knew that the show had just begun. Heavy bombers began flying over London for the first time, studying the ground but dropping no bombs. For a week the *blitz* seemed to stop and start every other day. Then on the twenty-second or twenty-third, bombs began to fall in London suburbs for the first time. Finally the mass bombing began in earnest, each day more intensive than the last, until by the sixth of September, people stopped counting air-raid warnings and the cables referred only to "constant alarms." But the real thing had still not begun.

At three o'clock in the afternoon of the seventh it happened. It was a fine late summer day. The air was clear. There had been a lull. Then suddenly out of nowhere they came by the hundreds, flying close together in formations so tight that the English pilots tell me they marveled at the technique. One pilot who had brought down four German planes told me he would "never have the nerve to fly in such close formation. Sure to bump into somebody, you know."

There were hundreds and hundreds and hundreds of them, layer upon layer. A moving picture taken from behind the machine guns of an English plane diving into such a formation is nightmarish. The screen is a solid block of planes flying so evenly that they look as if they were running on rails. They filled the English fighter's range finder because he was diving smack into the middle of them at 400 miles an hour. His eight streams of tracer bullets literally sprayed them—and they went flying on past as if on parade. In another film I saw of such an attack the formation was just beginning to break up when the pilot released his trigger and shut off the film. He could not have been more than 100 yards away from the German formation.

On Saturday, September 7, these fleets came in over London in such steady succession that the diving British pilots emptied their magazines and their gas tanks and went down to refuel and reload and came up to fight again. It was during these successive days of fighting that "The General" in *PM* began to worry about RAF pilot fatigue. He was quite right to worry. Six weeks later I was in a squadron hut when an RAF pilot read a newspaper account praising the command's heroism for attacking against odds of three and four to one. He read it out loud and everyone laughed.

"Wouldn't it have been fun in September," he said, "if we'd ever had a chance to fight with only three or four planes to one of ours?" The odds in individual battles over London at that time were more nearly ten or twenty to one. And the English were shooting them down in the air just the way the English and the French used to mow down German mass infantry attacks in the last war. And just as on the ground in the last war, in the air in this, the waves kept coming on—until September 15.

On the first day, the day when it began about three in the afternoon, the city by dusk was on fire with a hundred flames to guide the bombers that came in continuing waves through the night—through the black night in which the Spitfires and the Hurricanes cannot fight, when the game of bombing a twenty-five-mile-square city stops being a battle and becomes target practice with the barn door for a target.

This September 7 was the day that *PM*'s London correspondent, Ben Robertson, happened to choose to ride out of the city with Edward R. Murrow of Columbia Broadcasting System and Vincent Sheean, to sit on a haystack on a hill looking over the city. A few miles from their hilltop they stopped for a drink at a pub. When they came back they thought they'd stop for another. There wasn't any pub. With the bombs still dropping around him in London on that terrible night Robertson wrote the story that appeared in *PM* on September 9. No reconstruction of that day and night can match his account on the field—or Murrow's broadcast over the Columbia chain.

After I had been in London a week, I was sitting drinking beer in their apartment with the two extremely intelligent young men in respective charge of the two fire districts of the city of London—the east and the west side of the river. Ben Robertson was with me. He asked one of them how in the world they ever got the fires out that night. One fire chief looked at the other and grinned. Then he thought for a minute and said quite seriously, "I was extremely surprised when they did go out."

The water mains in England, where they do not have the heavy freezes we in the northeast of America have, tend to be laid close to the surface. During those nine terrible days in September they were smashed right and left, all over town. Nor was fire fighting in London as drilled and organized and veteran as when I saw and marveled at what is now without any doubt the most brilliant and able fire-fighting organization the world has ever known. It does not keep track of little fires. Of the big fires it *has* kept track of since the *blitz* began, there have been over 20,000.

The day after the seventh the fires were hardly out and the Germans came again. The streets were full of rubble, blown up from direct hits, filled with glass and brick and furniture, plaster, piping, and what-have-you from houses blown down. Whole telephone exchanges were out all over town. In almost continual raiding there is no time to clear or repair. Streets, avenues, districts are simply roped off and abandoned. No traffic—neither fire engines nor ambulances—can get through.

When I reached London a detour around a bomb crater or bomb damage was very much the exception rather than the rule—and more often than not simply avoiding a block from which an unexploded time bomb was being removed. In that agony in September, in the bombed areas, the clear street was almost the exception. And most of the work of the people who kept London alive and together, who put out its fires and dug out its wounded, who shepherded its people, had to be done at night in the inky and echoing black—unless by the light of the fires that made such excellent marks for successive waves of Heinkels.

It is no wonder that Adolf Hitler stamps and raves at the psychopathic British. It must be difficult for such a coward to understand such courage. It's extremely difficult for anyone to understand it. But it happened. The Londoners stuck it out without panic, each day burying their dead and binding up their wounded, each day going back to their businesses, unloading their boats in the middle of it all on the bombed docks, opening their stores, putting out their fires and repairing their telephone lines and water mains, shoveling out their streets, going back to their factories.

What no one will ever know now, thank God, is whether even the English could have taken it for longer than those nine days. Most of the most observant, informed, and intelligent people with whom I talked don't believe they could have. They believe that, *at that time*, another few days of continuous mass daylight raids and the fires would have been inextinguishable, the streets really impassable, important leaders would have been killed, the population finally shell-shocked into flight or submission.

When it ended, as I have said, no one knew it was over. No one—neither the government nor the people nor the firemen nor the police nor the air-raid-precaution departments nor the RAF. By that time, after nine twenty-four hours in succession, there was only continuous effort. There was no scorekeeper to tell anyone whether they were gaining ground or losing it. Just continuous accumulative destruction—just short of, never quite reaching, chaos.

The pilot I talked most with about the fight on the

last day, the fifteenth, is an American. He comes from Los Angeles. He had gone over to fight in France, got out to join the RAF. He had had several hundred hours on light planes in America. On September 15 he'd flown a pursuit ship only for thirty. The morning had been light. When he came down at noon, he thought he was through for the day. He was stepping out of his plane when the orders came to go back up. He said he didn't know it was a big show until he came over London at about 20,000 feet. Then he looked around him and saw the sky full of English planes.

Then he said he knew something big was going to happen that day. The sky was broken up with cumulous clouds, good cover for bombers. He'd been circling only a few minutes when the Germans came down out of these clouds—both bombers and fighters, by the hundred. He was in formation, watching the wing tip of a friend of his on the right. Suddenly smoke began to stream out of his partner's motor. He said to me, "The first time you see a friend of yours killed it kind of stuns you." He sat and watched him spin down on fire without thinking about the German planes. I asked him why his friend didn't jump. He said, "When it's coming back at you that hot you can't get out."

He was still looking down when he saw a Heinkel bomber below him which was heading toward a cloud. He kicked himself over into a dive, shot the bomber down just before it reached the cloud. He didn't remember much more of what happened or know why nobody had shot him while he sat there paralyzed, watching his friend burn. He just recalls that the sky had more planes in it than he had ever seen in one sky before, all hopelessly mixed up, and that it wasn't much trouble to find someone to shoot at.

After he'd run out of ammunition he came down and reloaded and climbed all the way back up again and it was still going on. At night when it stopped, the official score was 185 German planes down. The pilots in the RAF sincerely believe the real score was around 240. They had administered the *Luftwaffe*'s first major defeat.

There were no more big fights until the twenty-sixth and twenty-seventh—and the RAF won both hands down. There have been no more big fights since. The most characteristic sight of London by day is a sidewalk full of people going peacefully about their business, watching for busses, stopping to look in shopwindows, unhurried, apparently unconcerned. Nobody pays much attention to the lone raiders that come by day. People duck only if a plane swoops or a bomb whistles.

Bombers still come by night, and each morning there are a few less of London's millions and millions of buildings standing. But the true Hitlerian *Blitzkrieg*—the sudden, sharp defeat of a people by the simultaneous application of force and terror—has failed. It is probable, to repeat, that in the nine days in early September Hitler had practically won. What stopped him—fear, bewilderment, or lack of resources—it will be a long time before we know. But I give this as my carefully weighed opinion: on the last day of the battle over London he lost the only chance he will ever have to *Blitzkrieg* the British into submission.

There may be other ways he can conceivably beat the British. If he could bully or persuade the United States to withdraw its support he could wear the British down over a period of time. But he will never *Blitzkrieg* the people who have fought and lived in England through September. The *Blitzkrieg*, as he knows well, does not kill many people. Much more than half its force is fear. In all this holocaust in London—a city of eight million souls—not more than six thousand were killed during September from the air. Relatively few are maimed, for, characteristically, a bomb either kills you or it doesn't.

Hitler's weapon of terror buckled and broke when he struck at the British with it. It's no good any more. He has other weapons in his arsenal, but terror was far and away his best.

That Hitler's terror has failed is not simply my opinion, but is capable of proof on scientific evidence which I will set down presently.

The biggest news that I bring back from England is that it's now known that in the month of September Hitler took London and lost it because he failed to follow up the advantage that nine days of practically continuous mass raiding had given him. And that having failed to follow up his advantage he lost his opportunity to win the kind of *Blitzkrieg* that took Poland and Norway and Holland and Belgium and France for him. The RAF that beat him on September 15, and kept him beaten on the twenty-sixth and twenty-seventh, would like to see him try! From now on he must find some other way to win his infamous war.

I MEET THE WAR

I MET THE WAR in Lisbon up two flights of stairs—in a plain house on a steep and narrow street overlooking the harbor. That is, not counting Bermuda, where they pull down the shades when the Clipper flies over the island, to keep passengers from spying and where they are very grim and serious about passports and papers and censors. But in Bermuda somehow it's play. In Lisbon in the little room above the Rue de Sacramento, people crowd around the air attaché who must give permission for the 700-mile flight into England, and it's the real thing.

Here you meet your first war word—"priority"—and feel for the first time the seriousness with which the trip is taken. For you learn there are not two or three or ten other people who want to make the trip but several hundred. Officers, diplomats, couriers, commissions from the U. S., military observers, journalists—everything except businessmen. To go, one must have priority, and businessmen do not get priority in wartime.

The planes from Lisbon to London do not fly on any schedule. They go when they can. Big flying boats take off at dawn from the same pier that lands you from America. Or land planes taxi across an airport fifteen miles away, side by side with Fokker trimotors with enormous swastikas painted on their tails, bound for Berlin. You are told there is much mystery about when the British commercial planes go and from what airport. But long before you leave Lisbon gossip has told you when and where every British plane is and who's to be on board. Lisbon and its refugees and its gossip is a story of its own.

When you get to Lisbon, bound for London, you are interested only in a place on a plane—which suddenly seems impossible. The hours that matter are spent composing cables to people at home who don't understand the meaning of the word priority in a world whose business is war—and in trying to impress an air attaché who has a natural suspicion of journalists.

It is 3:30 in the morning you are called. The taxi arranged for the night before takes you out over the cobblestones to the river-harbor front at the edge of town. You have left your camera behind because the British will not carry it, even sealed. You begin to be apprehensive before you get into the plane because it is still dark and you think of the long flight ahead through enemy-infested air.

The ship I flew in was the *Clare,* just taken off its transatlantic run. Inside, it had been stripped of all its soundproofing and insulation. While we sat on the water in the harbor a steward came aft and explained to us how to take the seat cushions and make them into life preservers. His pupils were Lord Lothian, returning English Ambassador to America, three U. S. army aviators in mufti, a Swiss diplomatic courier, an unidentified lady who was Somebody, and myself. We were very attentive. I wondered whether the ship was armed but did not feel like asking. It wasn't.

The ship could have seated a couple of dozen more passengers but the whole forward half of it was piled high with mailbags—mailbags with labels showing that they came from all over the world. From Egypt, Australia, South America, and the U. S., from Canada and Spain and Switzerland. Lisbon is the great air-mail junction of the world, and here was news from the whole empire converging on London.

The sky was just light when we took off to the east, climbed above the hills that rise from Lisbon's peninsula, turned north over a barren countryside. I wondered how near we were to the enemy frontier.

The night before you fly to London you are apt to sit up because you suddenly find you don't like to say good-by to new-made friends. I fell asleep as we rose over the clouds just by the edge of the sea. When I woke up it was very cold. There was no land in sight. We were flying below a thin, broken layer of clouds and the two aviators in the seat opposite me were speculating on whether the clouds were thick enough to make cover for us. It was obvious why the pilot flew where he did, for even thin and scattered clouds above us screened us from any planes flying higher. We were only a thousand or two thousand feet above the water. From time to time we passed over small ships moving north and south.

In a straight line the flight may be made in five or six hours. We were in the air eight and a half. We must have swung 500 miles west of the mainland and come in a great circle into England. We figured that was what we were doing from the movement of the sun. We were cold all the time. It wasn't very rough. In the middle of the day the steward gave us hot coffee and a light lunch.

We kept looking out the window, appraising the cloud cover and expecting to see enemy aircraft. This was because none of us except the Swiss courier had made the trip before. He made it half a dozen times quite uneventfully. Later on I could find no record of any of these British commercial planes having been shot at or pursued in their trips back and forth to Lisbon. The only German plane reported—some months ago—had mistaken the flying boat for a fighting craft and hustled itself off over the horizon.

After a long time the skipper came down and told us we would be in at 4:30 in the afternoon. At 2:30 the steward made the rounds and shut up every window in the plane. He took squares of board and fastened them to the windows by suction cups. The last two hours were uncomfortable because every time the plane changed its course I could not keep myself from thinking that an enemy plane had been sighted. Presently we could hear rain on the wings and in a topsy-turvy world it was reassuring. It meant that the visibility must be bad.

Coming in to land we banked steeply, then slid smoothly onto water so calm that we knew it was in a harbor. There was some conversation about where we were landing, for we had not yet been told. We thought surely our port was in Wales or northern England. When the door opened at last and the cutter came up I asked the steward. We were on the southern coast of England directly across the channel from German-held France. I'm not going to name the town because while hundreds know it and on my way back I heard it quite casually referred to in a restaurant in Lisbon, I see no reason for giving it to the Germans in print.

On the dock there were soldiers in tin helmets, carrying rifles with fixed bayonets. Two dozen townsfolk watched us land with that same blankly curious look that airport crowds have on their faces the world over. In the few feet between the dock and the customs office I saw a harbor in which several good-sized cargo boats were being unloaded by cranes. There was no observable scar on this southern port of entry into Britain and the harbor life seemed completely normal. I felt very glad to be ashore.

All the sensations of the first twenty-four hours in England in war are exciting. Sensations that are commonplace later are new and intense. The good Lord Lothian excepted (representatives of the foreign office met him), all the passengers from the flying boat were herded into a small room whose windows were painted black and which already contained a dozen men in different kinds of uniforms. I never identified them all but most were probably home guardsmen. Home guardsmen are everywhere in England and very zealous in performance of their duties—usually relieving the regular army of guard details.

An airline steward served us tea and we were very cheerful and talked a lot. It felt like war again when, one by one, we were taken in to a still-smaller room and seated facing two civilian officials. The opening question to me was blunt: "Why are you here?" I told them I was the editor of a paper in New York and had a correspondent in London but I had come to see for myself —because the success of the war for Britain was so important to Americans and it was so difficult to form an accurate impression from so far away.

This argument appealed to neither of them and we went over it a good many times in different ways. One of them did not like a Spanish visa on my passport. The Pan American people in New York had insisted upon it in case of a forced landing in a Spanish port. The official wanted to know if I had ever been to Spain and didn't I have relatives there? The other asked for all my money and we counted it and he gave me a paper listing it. He explained that I could take no more than the amount of money I had out of the country when I left, or more than ten English pounds anyway. (I had mostly American money.)

All the time we talked—twenty or twenty-five minutes —one of them made a record of the conversation. Finally they gave me the money back, told me when I got to London I must report to the police right away, and let me go. Later on I got very used to being cross-questioned by policemen and censors, but for an American the first experience is sobering and a little unpleasant.

After the interrogation there was a long wait as the unidentified lady who was Somebody apparently had a really bad time of it and came downstairs in an English version of a dither. During the course of sitting around I had gathered that I had a choice of taking a train to London that night or staying in a near-by hotel and going up the next morning. The Swiss courier said I would be foolish to take a train since it would dump me in London late at night and taxis would be hard to find. Not having tried traveling in a blackout I took his advice on faith and was driven in a company car to the hotel. Ten miles of looking out the window. No visible damage. The rain had stopped, the traffic seemed normal, and we got to the hotel just before dark.

My first experience with a blackout was gentle. The American aviators and I decided to try it. The panes of the revolving door of the hotel were painted black. It had got dark while we were arranging for rooms and having a drink. Outside, in the streets of the provincial town, the sensation was eerie rather than frightening.

My hotel in London had a black, revolving door. I think I shall always remember the sensation of its spinning me out into the dark. One second you are in a cheerful, normally lighted hotel lobby full of pleasant sounds and talking people. Next—just as if you had fallen through a trap door—you are in pitch black. You feel it most in your feet because you don't know where to put them for the next step. Your eyes are unused to such complete darkness and see nothing. You put out your hands and you feel—outside most hotel doors—sandbags. Or the coats of unidentified people.

That first night the three aviators and I stood together for a few minutes getting used to it. My memory is of the clatter and echo of people walking and of somebody whistling gaily on the other side of the street in the dark. Presently the footsteps made some sense. Clearly there was a squad of soldiers in hobnail boots somewhere about, some women walking slowly on high heels, some men moving briskly. Swish! Swish! That would be two automobiles passing. The automobiles had hardly any lights—one headlight blacked out, the other fitted with a slotted hood that threw a tiny flashlight beam a few feet ahead of it on the pavement. And red taillights. But popped out into blackout for the first time, these lights didn't register for a few seconds.

Finally little illuminated Xs, marking obstructions in the roadway, emerged. We felt our way cautiously across the street. A bus loomed up, shifted gears, and moved past us. We were not very brave adventurers. We walked a block and a half, decided we might get lost, found our way back quite easily.

The sounds of many people walking in the street in a blackout is characteristic of provincial towns, quite uncharacteristic of London. If an air-raid warning had come, the footsteps would have hurried, then disappeared. None came.

We had an excellent dinner.

Later in my room I found such a large, stern sign warning me not to touch the heavy fastenings over the window that I slept without opening them. In the morning I was annoyed with myself for not having reasoned that once I had the lights out I could have unfastened the hangings and opened the windows to my heart's content.

The last day I was in England I caused a near riot because I had the window open, woke up in the middle of the night, and turned on the light for 30 seconds to see what time it was. Then I went back to sleep. A policeman spotted the light and was for waking up the whole hotel to find out who had made it. I learned of this at breakfast the next morning without letting on. You don't have to have the bad luck to be spotted by a policeman to get in trouble with a light at night anywhere in England. Show a light and the most casual passer-by will bellow at you, his voice echoing. After air raids have ceased to be simply a spectacle you will not need to be bellowed at. You will find you have a strong disinclination to showing a light by which an aviator might steer his way over your head.

In the morning the American aviators and I hired a car to drive to London because we thought we could see more of the countryside that way.

We left at eight o'clock in the morning. Our bags were packed on the roof of an old Daimler car, and the four of us rode in back. We had landed in England, been there overnight, heard no air raids, seen no enemy planes or damage from bombs. We decided we would keep track of what we were able to see on the drive. Two of us took one side and two the other. Up to what we decided was a definite entrance to London—the city as distinct from its suburbs—we counted exactly thirteen "confirmed" hits. Four of these were craters in fields. Only one of them was damage to a working place, although traveling a main highway from the coast through southern England we passed at least a score of factories, sandbagged and with spotters on the roofs. We joked more and more about bomb damage as we went along— until we got into the center of London.

From the minute we started we were all eyes. The old Daimler rolled along slowly—at thirty or thirty-five miles an hour, down a road with few civilian cars on it, army trucks passing us sometimes in groups of a dozen or more, soldiers on motorcycles, civilians on bicycles. Almost immediately we began passing through tank traps, usually concrete abutments on either side of the road, with 500-pound cylindrical blocks of concrete with great rings set in the top piled by the side of the road, for hauling out onto the highway. On either side of the emplacements on the road there would be ditches or barbed wire or concrete poles set in the ground—fanning out twenty or thirty feet. They did not seem to me very substantial. I asked the army men with me about this. They said that all the defenders cared about was to force the tanks off the road into the open country. They also pointed out to me new-laid pavement on either side of the tank trap—cobblestones or packed dirt. "Mined," they said.

In the fields on either side of the more pretentious traps were circles of barbed wire a hundred yards or more in diameter. There was evidence of something purposeful in the center of each—sandbagged breastworks or camouflage. "Strong points," said my military friends. They are scattered about so that the machine guns in each can enfilade troops attacking any of the others. In some places there were concrete blockhouses with slots through which to fire.

Soon we began to pass fields in which there were all manner of strange goings on. One would be crisscrossed irregularly with ditches—not deep enough to be trenches. Or alternating ditches and mounds, obviously made by a heavy scraper digging down a foot or more as it ran along for a hundred yards and then piling its dirt aboveground for another few yards, then going back to dig. We figured these were to destroy the fields for landing enemy aircraft. In other fields there were scores and scores—perhaps hundreds—of heavy posts set irregularly twenty or thirty feet apart. Across others battered wrecks of cars had been scattered as if flung by the giant handful.

It was a beautiful autumn day with only a few fleecy

clouds above. The towns through which we passed were filled with people going about their business—on the highway, with much honking of horns. A few of the towns—not all—had the beginnings of street barricades of bricks. Shoppers walked around them. Every few miles we would pass a camp of some kind. We could not tell for what purpose they all were meant, although scattered through one we saw little tanks, camouflaged. One we recognized as on the edge of an airfield, although it was beyond a hedgerow and we could see no planes. We recognized it because its shape was right for an airfield and because in one corner, snuggled half into the ground and half behind sandbags, was a heavy machine-gun nest, the nose of the gun pointed skyward. We could just see the helmets of the crew. They were looking upward.

All antiaircraft-gun emplacement crews look a little like enlarged toy soldiers, for they are always looking up, quite immobile. They must always look up, for it only takes a few seconds for a plane to dive out of the clouds. The aviators with me kept hearing the noise of planes flying. None of the passers-by or soldiers in the fields paid any attention.

Presently the road began to run under a series of regularly spaced contraptions made of iron piping. On either side of the road were pairs of pipes, perhaps twenty feet high, parallel to the road, stuck in the ground fifteen feet apart, their tops crossed in the air. Laid in this cross was another pipe that bridged the road. The whole apparatus was held in place with guy wires out to the side. I diagnosed these as devices to keep enemy planes from landing on the highway. The American Army corrected me. They were standard signal-corps preparations for laying field-telephone lines under fire. Should the signal corps have to lay wires across the road while troops were using it lengthwise—and lay them in a hurry—they had simply to hoist their wires up over the traffic onto one of these light bridges.

The officers explained to me that one would have to know the terrain intimately to understand the method to all this. Defenses—obstructions, strong points, etc.—would be arranged so as to make use of the terrain. One's own army must be able to move rapidly and yet the enemy must be hindered by cross fire, mines, traps, and the natural obstructions of rivers, woods, and hills.

Closer to London, where the road chose to widen and run straight, we did come upon devices to prevent enemy aircraft landing on the highway. These turned out to be lengths of concrete sewer piping set on end ten or fifteen feet high, in regularly spaced rows on either side of the paving.

During all the first half of our trip civilian and military life was hopelessly intertwined. Each seemed to be going about its respective business without disturbance to or consciousness of the other. Motorcycle dispatch riders plowed through bicyclists; delivery trucks and armored cars followed one another in line; here was a field of barbed wire, there a field of truck gardening. Only at one point where the road swung parallel to the south coast for a few miles did we see roads barricaded off with sandbags and barbed wire and guarded with sentries—evidence of zones wholly forbidden to civilians.

As we came nearer to London the activity of soldiers lessened, dwindled, finally disappeared. The suburbs began to eat up the countryside. Traffic became heavier and almost wholly civilian. We had passed through the defenses of the south coast.

The trip took a little over three hours. It was halfway over before we noticed the most characteristic thing of all: the complete absence of clues as to where we were. At the crossroads there are no signposts whatever, but this is only the beginning. In each town wherever, on a sign or the glass window of a store front, the name of the town or the county might have been revealed, it was carefully painted out. Even the commercial trucks on the road had addresses and telephone numbers conspicuously painted out. England's roads are complicated things. Later, even when I was driving with officers who had grown up in the country, we were continually getting lost or stopping every little while to ask directions of a passer-by. I always found that directions were cheerfully given, but I was told that this co-operation was simply evidence that the September invasion scare had passed.

On our long drive into London, the houses that we'd seen which had been hit by bombs had been damaged, rather than demolished—a front blown out, windows shattered, etc. It was not until we got toward the center of London that we began to see buildings not damaged but demolished.

By the time the drive to London was over I was feeling very chipper. The warlike countryside, with its machine-gun strong points, its tank traps, and its sentries with bayonets in their rifles, had been extremely interesting and the lack of damage from bombs on the ground or any enemy aircraft in the air was completely reassuring. I remember thinking that if it were not quite "all a newspaper story," the whole thing was very much exaggerated. It was elating to be in London at last—what with stopovers in Bermuda and waiting for the plane in Lisbon I had been ten anxious days on my way. It had been five years since I had been in London. The city as I came into it looked very much the same. The streets seemed busy and peaceful.

The first sobering sensation was the score of bomb damage my aviator companions were keeping. At what we decided was the edge of London proper—having chalked up thirteen hits in well over a hundred miles of motoring—we began a new score. We had not gone half a mile before the new score was double the old and for the first time we saw gaps between rows of houses—gaps where other houses had been. Bomb damage is freakish in extreme. I shall come back to talk of it. But when I refer to a building in London as having been demolished by a bomb I do not mean damaged or made uninhabitable or partially destroyed or even in ruins. By demolished I mean demolished. Here where a house stood, its rooms furnished, its walls papered, and its plumbing intact, clothes in its closets and carpets on its floors, cooking utensils in the kitchen and toothbrushes in its bathrooms, shades on its windows and a roof overhead—here where all these things were there is but nothing. Literally nothing. There is no pile of ruins. Underneath the nothing it is flat. It is a filled-in hole in which what was this house is pulverized into such small pieces that the pieces are indistinguishable.

I am still talking about a house that's been demolished. Of all the houses that are bomb damaged in London there are relatively few that are demolished. But when they are demolished they are exactly as I have described. As you stand looking at the place the house was —or ride past it as I did that first day, looking out the window—you see only the bottom of the nothing where the house was and in this bottom there seems to be nothing bigger than the size of two fists put together; and of all the things that are packed into this bottom to nothing the only recognizable shape seems to be of broken bricks.

It is this pulverization of a house that produces the correspondent's word *rubble*. The first question that George Lyon, the managing editor of *PM*, asked me when I got back was what correspondents mean when they cable that the streets are filled with rubble. This is what they mean. Rubble is pulverized human dwelling. It is very dusty. People who are lucky enough to walk out of a house in which rubblizing has taken place emerge as if they had crawled out of a flour bin.

It was between the edge of the city proper and my hotel that I first saw places where buildings had been demolished. One does not take in the significance of demolition at first sight. For the reason I have explained: one does not see a ruin. One sees nothing—and so is unable to visualize what was there before the conversion to nothing happened.

This phenomenon produces a standard London joke: about the young lady who had just come to town and whose guide pointed to a break in a row of buildings, explaining, "That's where a bomb dropped last night." Said the young lady, "Oh, but wasn't it lucky that the bomb missed all those houses and fell in that vacant lot."

And so on my first morning in London it was not the extent of damage to any one place that surprised or shocked me—because I couldn't take it in. I remember this very distinctly. It was simply the fact that having counted only thirteen bomb incidents in over a hundred miles I now counted thirty in half a mile. It simply dawned on me gradually that here something had really happened.

I left the American aviators, with whom I had journeyed from Lisbon, at another hotel and proceeded to the Dorchester. I went to the Dorchester because another traveler, the Swiss courier, had told me that several people I wanted to see were staying there. I went there despite a warning from a man I'd met in Lisbon that I should avoid the Dorchester like a plague because it fronted on a park and London's parks are inhabited by antiaircraft batteries that shake the buildings around them and inhibit sleep. I got there a little before noon.

III

ALARM

I WAS SO EXCITED my first day in London that I felt as if I were burning. I wanted to see everything and talk to everybody at once.

The wire I had sent Ben Robertson when I landed the day before got to him the day after I arrived. But I had had a telephone conversation with a representative of the Ministry of Information and had asked him to reserve me a room at the Dorchester. It was a good thing I had, because the hotels in London are full. None of the larger or better known of them has been bombed out,* but so many government officials who used to live in the country now stay in town and so many of the better-off people in London *have* been bombed out and moved into the nearest hotel that there are few empty hotel rooms in town.

The Dorchester is a modern eight-story building—high for London—facing Hyde Park, to the west, across Park Lane. My rooms, a bathroom, a bedroom with twin beds and a sitting room, arranged in that sequence, were on the seventh floor with a magnificent view over the city.

* Bombed out: technical slang universally used in London. It means, variously, either "rendered uninhabitable"—if used about a building—or "driven out of one's quarters"—either living or working —if used about an individual family or group of people.

At night while I lived there I made the bath into a dark-
room, out of which window I could watch the fireworks
while there were people and lights in the other rooms.
When I arrived I looked out of the wide windows and
saw the balloon barrage for the first time. I had not seen
it as I drove into London, although that is probably
because I was in a closed car. I do not know what other
people who have only read of the balloon barrage imagine it's like but I had always thought of it as a ring of
balloons around the outskirts of the city.

In London, it is no ring at all. Balloons shoot up all
over the city like stalks of a badly planted asparagus bed.
That first day scores of them floated over the city in the
sunlight, here, there, there, here, there. I guessed they
were about 4000 feet up—three Empire State Building-
lengths. They all rested at about the same altitude.

The balloons themselves have a front and a rear, the
rear drooping down like Jimmy Savo's pants. When you
see them go up in the morning, as you often do, the rear
or baggy-pants part hangs down deflated and they wabble
and yaw on their lines as they go up. As they get higher
they settle down and the pressure of the air becomes less
and the back-of-the-pants part inflates until, at full altitude, it stands out, awkward but stiff. It acts as a kind of
rudder and all the balloons point in the same direction,
as cows do in a field on a windy day. Their arrangement
in the sky, except for the fact that they are the same
height, makes no sense and changes every day. For the
balloons themselves go up from trucks which move about,
so that the incoming dive bombers will not know where
to expect them. Balloon officers who are very serious
about their work refer to it happily as flying—much to
the disgust of the RAF with whom they and their gear
are almost as unpopular as the utility companies that put
up high-tension lines next to airports are to commercial
fliers in peaceful countries. Every once in a while in a

fog a member of the RAF runs into one of their cables, or almost does.

Although *PM*'s Ben Robertson was not there to meet me I was pretty sure he would show up for lunch. I decided I had time to see what "registering with the police" was like. I thought I might get the Ministry of Information to do it for me, but that it would be more interesting to walk in cold. I went down to have the doorman call a taxi. The doorman was in livery. He stood on the curb just outside two enormous abutments of sandbags piled around the entrance of the hotel. I asked the liveried doorman and the taxi driver whom he called where the nearest police station was—or the one that aliens should register at. This sounded like a simple question, but it wasn't. It appeared that the right police station had been bombed out the day before yesterday. The conference was enlarged to include the traffic officer on the corner. He confirmed the bombing out, but did not know where the police station had gone. He ventured to suggest that the station that had been hit had been a new one to which the records had just been moved from an older establishment that was not thought to be safe. He suggested that possibly they had gone back to the original quarters. He proved to have been correct.

The place of registration was no ordinary police station, but temporary quarters consisting of a long counter behind which six or eight extremely busy policemen sat facing equally busy and much more anxious aliens who seemed to have a tendency to shift from one foot to another and lean across the counter to explain things. Behind the policemen were tier on tier of files over which a half a dozen more policemen were climbing, standing on chairs, opening and shutting drawers. A mourners' bench ran along the remaining wall and I was seated at one end to wait my turn. The queue moved up slowly, edging along the bench.

I was almost at the top of the line when the first air raid came. I did not hear the siren—most of the time when you are indoors you do not hear the siren. A policeman from the street simply stuck his head in the door and blew like hell on a police whistle. I jumped a mile. The room was suddenly still. The sergeant in the middle of the counter chanted in a monotonous voice without looking up:

"An air-raid alarm has been sounded. There is a shelter underneath this building. The man at the door will show you the way to it. If you do not choose to go to the shelter we will carry on."

Nobody went. The buzz of conversation resumed. I thought everyone was very brave, myself included. Later I found out that no one in London ever pays any attention to daylight raids unless he is on the street and hears the plane directly overhead or sees it diving toward him.

Telephone switchboards occasionally shut down for a few minutes following the alert. There does not seem to be a rule about this. Sometimes they do and sometimes they don't. I never found that they would not take a call within a few minutes afterwards, however.

On the street when the siren goes during the day people are apt to look up into the sky without breaking their stride. If there is anything going on up there a certain number of people will stop on the street corners or lean back against the buildings and watch. Other people walking by will look up from time to time out of the corner of one eye. By something going on I mean planes whose exhausts are visible or particularly interesting antiaircraft puffs. An occasional burst of antiaircraft is not worth neck craning and the show has to be fairly entertaining to hold its crowd for more than a few minutes.

Within a few minutes after my first whistle had made me jump the continued buzz of quiet activity reassured me and my heart stopped beating so loudly. But life was definitely more interesting than it had been before the alert sounded.

The cop who registered me when my turn came was very cheerful. He had relatives who lived in Connecticut. He said he had been meaning to visit them for years.

Because the cop was so cheerful, filling out the forms went merrily. What the police got were the particulars of my passport, where I intended to live, what I intended to do, and where I intended to go. What I got was a small cardboard folder about three by four inches in which my picture was presently pasted—I was required to submit two prints of my passport likeness, which I eventually had to go back to the hotel to get. And last, another and slightly smaller cardboard folder called an identity card and a food-rations book with tickets for two weeks.

The folder with my picture in it I used a good deal and was required to show at hotels and several times in the process of arranging for an admission to government buildings. They took it away from me boarding the plane when I checked out of the country. I did not use my food book. It said something in small type about presenting it at hotels, and at each hotel I visited I was given literature which advised me to submit my food book at the end of my stay. But when the times came for me to pay my bills, nobody ever asked me for it. I held on to it hoping to bring it home, but they took that too just before I got on the plane.

The identity card seemed to me to duplicate the registration card with my picture on it but whenever I presented it instead of the latter it was brushed aside. Not even the man who took the registration and the food book from me at the end of my stay wanted it and I do not know yet why it was given to me.

Of the three documents, the unused food book was most interesting. It was about four by six inches, printed on cheap paper, and contained a dozen or more leaves. After a page or two of instructions it consisted of solid pages of small coupons, the coupons on each page successively labeled "Sugar, Butter and Cooking Fats, Bacon, Meat." The whole booklet represented more than my quota for two weeks, so the policeman tore out the coupons I did not need before giving me the book.

The instructions told me to pick out the tradesmen with whom I wanted to do business and to register with them and to inscribe their names in blank places in my food-ration book. Then each day in my shopping for food these tradesmen were to tear out the coupons necessary to cover my purchases. It was explained to me that if I did not use up the allotted coupons in the allotted time their value expired. In other words I could not eat less this month in order to have more to eat next.

If there is any question about whether one starves in London I can report that I gained several pounds in weight while I was there. And the fact that no hotel asked for my food-ration book does not mean that I lived without benefit of rationing. Guests in hotels are served only rationed quantities. In terms of actual meals it works out this way:

SUGAR: Sugar is served individually, three small square lumps per person per meal. Most English apparently like more sugar than this and there is joking about the popularity of guests who take no sugar in their tea or coffee. But the hotel guest who uses his three lumps of sugar does not deny himself a sweet at the end of the meal—a pudding, a tart, an ice. The sweets served in the hotel did not seem to have as much sugar in them as similar dishes have at home. But the difference is small. My own particular racket when I felt my sweet tooth aching was to order a dessert that might require powdered sugar—like blackberries or rice pudding. The powdered sugar in shakers did not seem to be quotaed.

— 33 —

BUTTER: Like sugar, butter also comes individually served and like sugar in three very small parts. This is definitely not as much butter as I am used to eating at a meal. Each day at breakfast I debated with myself whether to eat two small pieces of toast, which is all that could be well buttered with the ration, or spread it thinner over four or five. (On the sugar-rationing side, by the way, marmalade for breakfast is still available. It did not mean much to me because I don't like it.)

BACON: The rationing is apparent in the fact that bacon and eggs come with two small strips of bacon, whereas I remember bacon and eggs in England used to mean two or three times this amount.

MEAT: The order of England is that in any given meal one may have a meat course or a fish course, but not both.

VOLUME: My own gain in weight is the best evidence I know. All the time I was in England I was very active. I walked four or five times as many miles daily as I ever do at home and slept less. I probably drank two or three highballs a day more than I do normally. I observed no quota on liquor. A meal of hors d'oeuvres, or soup, followed by a course of meat or fish and then dessert is certainly a fair meal, particularly since almost everywhere I went vegetables were served in variety and as many helpings as one liked. Also bread. At the Englishman's fourth meal—tea—he consumes more bread, cake, and pastry than I would guess many Americans eat in a day. At tea on a train, for instance, the waiter served a tray with four or five kinds of bread, cake, and pastry not twice, but three or four times, to almost everyone in the car except myself.

In the provincial towns I found the rationing in the hotels less strict than in London—the portions were larger and there was a definite tendency to leave how much bacon one took from a large platter up to the individual conscience.

While I was in England I ate in several different hotels, two restaurants, and one private house. I never ate alone, even at breakfast. I heard practically no conversation about rationing except the gentle joking about the sugar. Nor did I feel that the people I met and talked with felt the rationing either imposed or an imposition. I did feel—quite strongly—that people regarded the conservation of food as patriotic and I believe that it would be difficult for a man who took advantage of the laxness of the rationing regulations to keep his fellow countrymen's respect. But I cannot document this.

That first day in the police station when I got my food book I was fascinated with it. Within a few days I had forgotten all about it.

While the policeman was busy filling in forms and counting coupons we talked. After his long hours in the bureau he worked at night as a volunteer. His talk about his work at night did not make much sense to me then, for I didn't know how much work there is to be done at night in a city that is being bombed. Later, as I went about the city after dark, most of the men and women I met who were holding down responsible jobs—excepting in the Fire and Police Departments—were volunteer workers. That first day I did not know enough to be impressed by Patrolman McLean's cheerfulness. It was neither forced nor professional. It was simply free and easy. Just as we were finishing, the policeman at the door blew his whistle again and said, "All clear." Again nobody paid any attention to him.

When I got back to the hotel, Ben Robertson was waiting for me. I had not seen him since he left for London two weeks before we printed the first issue of *PM*. I had a lot to talk to him about and to learn from him. I thought we might spend a quiet afternoon planning the next few days there, have a quiet dinner at the end of my first day. It was then one o'clock in the afternoon. Exactly fourteen hours later I got to bed.

GAY BY DAY, GRIM BY NIGHT

I TOLD SOMEONE that the most striking aspects of London are the normalcy of life by day and the dramatic suddenness with which that life stops at sundown when the blackout begins. The two worlds, the world of peace and the world of war, exist side by side, separated by only a few moments of twilight. After you've been in London a little while this becomes commonplace. My first day in London I "couldn't get over it."

To begin with, meeting Ben Robertson for lunch in the Dorchester was so like meeting another friend for lunch had been the first day I arrived in London five years before. In the Dorchester there is a small lobby with the porter's desk and the clerks to the right and the cigarette and newsstand counter to the left. The lobby opens directly on a large room which is a foyer most of the day, furnished with comfortable chairs and tables. Half of it is cleared and set as a grill room for luncheon and dinner. Still farther beyond is the dining room proper where the tables have linen on them, and it is quieter. This dining room in turn leads off to the right into another dining room where there are a circular floor and a raised band platform and where people dance at night. The lobby, foyer-grill, dining room, and the place for dancing all really run together and are distinguished simply by what people do in them.

I describe these rooms in detail because I want you to see them as I saw them, first on the noon of a sunny fall day filled with busy people and then again as I saw them fourteen hours later, coming in out of the black from walking through shelters—coming in to the dull light with a steel helmet on my head, with the night guns echoing in my ears and blowing in the curtains, seeing the people sleeping in the corners, and meeting the weather-reddened, incendiary-bomb spotter coming down from the roof. With the liveried elevator man opening the door for him. Seeing the old lady who nightly makes a nest for herself of steamer rugs and pillows in the corner where the hors d'oeuvre stand rests by day. Sitting with my taxi driver unself-consciously drinking beer on the sofa where at noon I met Lady Diana Duff Cooper, looking as chic as a page from *Vogue* and making jokes with her friends.

Now at noon when I came first into these rooms there was no sign of war or siege except that a good many of the men and some of the women wore uniforms. The lobby was crowded with people coming and going, telephoning, buying papers, stopping to speak to each other. In the near end of the lobby groups were ordering cocktails and drinking them, interrupting each other, getting up and sitting down. Beyond, the tables were a crowded clatter. As in London in a fashionable restaurant five years ago, so in London that noon, more people knew each other than do in fashionable restaurants in New York. Ben stopped at almost every other table to introduce me to someone. I was news because I had just flown from New York and people were politely interested. No one asked me what New York was like, though a few wanted to know how I thought the election was coming out.

At lunch the menu seemed as bountiful as the menu of any international hotel, whether in London or New York or Buenos Aires. So did the wine list.

I sat and looked around me and could not believe it. It was rich, gay, cosmopolitan London unchanged.

I am recording what I saw and felt in the order that I saw and felt it. Later on you will see that my skepticism —my difficulty in believing the Dorchester at lunch was real—was not entirely unsound. But the Dorchester, and the life people live in it, are a definite part of the picture. As at the Dorchester, so at other hotels such as the Ritz and the Savoy. The sharp contrast of these hotels with life in the rest of London does not lessen with familiarity. The menus after you come to know them have perhaps less variety than you first recognized. The service in the dining rooms is not what it used to be, because so many good Italian waiters and maîtres d'hôtel have fled or are in concentration camps. But the English service above stairs—the valeting and the lady's maiding—is as conscientious and as thoughtful and as smoothly self-effacing as ever. And the whole is miraculously as it was.

I had come to London to see for myself what it was like. There were hundreds of questions in my mind— things I wanted to see, people I wanted to talk to. But principally, I wanted first to know whether there was more or less physical damage than I had gathered from the cables and the radio—nonmilitary damage and damage to vital military production. Once oriented on this score, I wanted to gather facts with which to make up my mind on how the war in the air was going. Who controlled the heavens over Britain, how able was the RAF in combating Goering's *Luftwaffe*, and how accurate were the communiqués? Then I wanted to go to the people of London as directly as a stranger might be able, to make up my mind from talking with them what the terrific experience of bombardment from the air was doing to them. Technically this is called studying civilian morale.

And finally, when I had done this elementary homework, I wanted to meet and talk with enough members of the government and people who had power of decision in crucial policies so that I might form opinions on several scores, such as: What were these people fighting for? Did they know? How were the Siege of London, the Battle of Britain, the War for the Empire going forward? And underlying all these questions, the biggest question of all: What evidence was there for or against the theory that real social issues were involved, that the war was or was not simply a war between two very small ruling classes, rivals for the right to exploit people at home and colonial empires abroad? And the practical aspect of that question: What possibility was there that the struggle for dominance in the world would end as the struggle over Czechoslovakia ended—in sudden conciliation and appeasement?

In the war or out, the American people are today behind the British Empire, their riches are at its service in fighting Fascism. So there was first the simple question of whether the British were winning or being beaten. And then the subtler and more complicated one of whether the war was on the up and up, whether it was an honest war against what was evil, or a dishonest war whose British makers would be quite willing to settle for the right to co-exist with Fascism or to make a Fascist state themselves and live as simply another gangster in a world governed by gangsterism.

I knew I could not get the answers to all these questions. I did not expect to get them and I have not got them. What I sought and what I got was firsthand evidence bearing on these questions—that firsthand evidence to be digested at leisure.

That you should understand both the extent and the limits of my evidence—and because it may not be uninteresting in itself—I write this diary of my experiences during two weeks which sometimes seem to me like a lifetime, because they were lived so intensely.

As I look back on it—I am writing a few days after my return—it seems to me that these two weeks could have been lived so intensely nowhere else, under no other circumstances. In the first place, to my surprise, in London I suddenly found that I had a reputation. My visit was taken with seriousness.

I don't believe that this was solely because *PM* has in its brief lifetime taken an aggressive anti-Fascist and generally pro-English point of view—coming out for the sale of the destroyers to Britain, frankly and honestly angry at the wanton bombing of London. That got me a letter of introduction from Lord Lothian to Prime Minister Churchill—and the extremely able and intelligent co-operation of the Ministry of Information, a wartime body which, among other things, operates a continuous, and startlingly frank, secret Gallup-poll operation appraising civilian morale.

To understand how it happened that I went beyond these amiable and orthodox formalities you must understand—and I'm afraid it will be very difficult for you, so far away from it—how alone these people feel, besieged upon an island from which they ran a world so long. And how their confidence in themselves has been tried. So that when a man came to them from America of his own free will and in friendliness—a man who is what they call a "newspaper owner" and thus presumably quite able to find out what he wants to know by sending his correspondents while he sleeps in his warm bed at home—they are not impressed by the gesture, but they are touched by it.

I am using the word "they" very inclusively, to include a Prime Minister, who made me an awkward little speech of thanks which embarrassed me very much, to the unknown air-raid warden trying to tell me his hopes and his problems, sitting in the cellar in the dark, to young pilots who came down from cold encounters with death at 400 miles an hour, six miles in the sky, to pedestrians on the street, and whoever it was who left the anonymous little note at the Dorchester which read:

> For neither despising us,
> Patronizing us,
> Nor advising us,
> Ingersoll of U. S. A.
> Earns a Briton's thanks today.

All this was often embarrassing, because one is not in London forty-eight hours before being extremely conscious of the fact that one is living with a people who are fighting for their lives—whether they fight by sleeping uncomfortably in a shelter so that they may work again tomorrow, or fight by putting out fires, or by sucking oxygen out of a mask so that they do not lose their depth perception when aiming machine guns at high altitudes. And one feels there is a quality of indecency in the eagerness of one's curiosity, an intrusion on something extremely personal and intimate of which one is not really a part.

But as a journalist—as a journalist as distinct from a human being—my position in England as the first American publisher to get myself on a plane and fly 3000 miles to see and talk and be with the British, meant that instead of snooping and prying and sparring for facts and information, I met no one anywhere in any walk of life who did not seem to feel that for the little time I was with him the most important thing in this world was to tell, explain, and show and make possible for me to see and hear what I wanted. Not—and this is most important —what he or she wanted me to see or hear—but what I wanted.

Not even in the Ministry of Information, whose job after all was to sell me Britain's point of view, did anyone anywhere try to sell me anything. Even my most challenging assertions—such as that enormous numbers of Americans believed the British government would still sell out its people and appease the Fascists—were met and discussed frankly and thoughtfully. So were expressions of skepticism that a democratic revolution was really taking place in England.

In the middle of my stay I cabled back to *PM* that I was being given complete freedom of action and was using it. I was given more than that. I felt as if I were being given the kind of co-operation that a Notre Dame halfback gets from the other ten men on his team when running off-tackle.

It's important here to say something about the American correspondents in London. They serve us here in America much better than we know—or at least much better than I thought any correspondents could. Not one of them who has worked in England through the *blitz*— using the word as the English use it, meaning events since the first of August—but knows infinitely more than I about practically everything I am writing about. The only thing that distinguishes my journalism from theirs is this: they have long since become a part of the show. They can and do tell us accurately day by day the news of what's going on in London. They are circumscribed— yes—but really much less than I find most Americans imagine. But the price that's paid for their knowledge and sophistication is their loss of the sense of the strange or the unusual, the strange or the unusual to the Americans at home. They are no longer sure of what Americans at home are curious about.

If I would revise foreign correspondence after a trip in the field, it would be with this prescription: that cables from editors to correspondents should be at least as long as from correspondents to editors. The American correspondents in London can tell us practically anything we want to know. But we don't know, because the American editors, including *PM*'s editor—speaking—have never asked them the questions, have never cabled, "This is how we over here imagine things are in England. Are we right or wrong?"

This is what sets the journalism of a flying trip like mine apart from the solid, sound, day-by-day journalism of the Ben Robertsons and the Helen Kirkpatricks and the Ed Murrows: that I went to England with a complete equipment of preconceived notions gained from imperfect knowledge and with a boxful of questions, the answers to which the Americans in London knew too well. And when I speak of the co-operation I got from everyone in England, the American correspondents are emphatically included. They were swell.

To complete my credentials I should add that one of my oldest and best friends, with whom I am connected by marriage, is an Englishman who returned to England after a career in this country and who is now a Wing Commander in the RAF. He is a Wing Commander in the RAF partially by virtue of the fact that twenty years ago he was in command of the most famous single fighter squadron in England, No. 56. Not the least of the courtesies extended me by the government was having Wing Commander Maxwell given four days' leave to show me the RAF. Much of what I have learned of aerial combat comes from him and from his twenty-two-year-old brother, Michael, currently a combat pilot in his brother's old squadron. With a private license and 160 hours in the air, I knew just enough about flying myself to be able to understand the language.

I have broken in on the diary of my first day in London with this long discussion about what it was I went to seek and how the English received me and the sources of the information I am presently to set down because it was on my first afternoon that I faced the problem of "what next?"

Ben and I sat in the drawing room of my suite and talked about it after lunch. The head of the Ministry of Information is Alfred Duff Cooper, whose wife is the former Lady Diana Manners. They lived in the Dorchester. They had asked us to dinner that night. Good.

The paper with the largest circulation—2,700,000—in Great Britain is called the *Daily Express*. It's owned by Lord Beaverbrook and editorially it's a cross between the New York *Daily News* and *Time* magazine—whose brand of journalism has always fascinated Beaverbrook. One of its "star reporters" is tiny, pert, pretty Hilde Marchant, a Yorkshire girl of inexhaustible energy and a terrierlike disposition. She is currently in charge of the *Express'* editorial campaign for the improvement of shelters. She rides by night in a company car, under a black-painted tin hat, and everyone in the shelter business knows, respects, and, if he is not on his job, fears her. Ben says she wants to meet me; she wants to show me the shelters herself before any officials from the Ministry of Home Security get hold of me and sell me a bill of goods. Fine. We'll get hold of her for tomorrow night.

I want to see Ed Murrow again, because I admire his broadcasts and want to find out how he goes about getting his information every day. We know we can find Murrow after midnight at the broadcasting station. Good. We'll get hold of him after dinner.

Now we must decide how to go about seeing people in

the government—whether to use the letters I brought with me from New York, the good offices of one or two old friends in London, or put it up to the Ministry of Information who Ben says will be my official host—in the person of one Douglas Williams, head of what's called "the American Section." I remembered that Williams, whom I had never met, had sent me a message of greeting when I landed from the plane.

It is still a fine, sunny afternoon, the noise of traffic along Park Lane, taxis honking and busses whirring, comes faintly through the open windows. The canopy of balloons over London catches gold from the sun as it drops toward the horizon. There could not be a more peaceful scene.

There is no indication that there is a war on—for nothing could be less warlike-looking than a flotilla of balloons. Until we start working the telephone.

The telephone in London is war inconvenience number one. The electricity, Ben tells me, has never been out for more than brief interludes. Now and then, in one section or another, the gas has gone for a little while. When I take my first bath I will find some rust coming up through the Dorchester's new plumbing because the bombs have jarred it loose from the old mains under the street—many of the mains in London are so old, I am told, that they are not on any maps. But the telephones seem the most vulnerable of the services. Whole exchanges are out for long periods. All the time I was there the Ministry of Information was able to call me, but I was never able to call the Ministry of Information back, because the exchange handled only outgoing calls—a phenomenon that never percolated to the Ministry's secretariat, which was continually leaving me polite requests to call back.

I did a great deal of telephoning in London. I would estimate that I completed about nine out of ten calls.

But the tenth always seemed to be someone I wanted to get hold of in a hurry. The telephone girls always said something like, "I don't believe you can get any Butterfield numbers today, but I will be glad to try, sir." Presently, they reported that they were sorry but they couldn't put the call through. Long distance is even more difficult. You wait anywhere from a few minutes to a few hours to have one completed. That is, unless you can establish priority. Important government business has an exchange of its own—with secret numbers—which always works. And on regular exchanges it has what's called "triple priority." Triple priority is magic.

I had a letter from Washington to Ambassador Joe Kennedy. At 4:30 I interrupted my telephoning to walk around the corner to the Embassy. Mr. Kennedy was returning to the United States next day. I talked with him for about half an hour and came back to the hotel. The sun was just going down, it was still light, but a cheerful, gray little maid was tugging heavy portieres across the windows. It felt odd to be sitting in a heavily curtained room with the lights all on when it was still light outside. Some people came in for a drink. Presently Ben looked at his watch and said, "They'll be here in about ten minutes." I said, "Who?" He said, "The Germans. They come every night about seven, now."

I had forgotten all about the Germans. The conversation went on. People were telling me stories—completely unreal stories—about what it was like in September. One man had had a German bomber crash into his house. Another said his had never been hit, but that it had cost him a total of nine pounds to keep the tiles on his roof repaired when pieces of antiaircraft shell kept falling on them and breaking one or two at a time. There was a little talk about what had been hit the night before. The conversation was unreal, but it excited me. The drawn curtains excited me, and the fact that Ben said "they" were coming soon. I didn't want to hear, I wanted to see for myself. I left them talking, went through the bedroom into the bathroom, and, leaving the lights out, found my way to the window. There was a heavy drape over it, but I crawled inside it as an old-fashioned photographer used to crawl under his camera hood to focus. I opened the French window.

The London of the balmy afternoon was gone and no cheerfully lighted city was there to take its place. A hundred yards away was utter and absolute pitch black. Directly below me a hooded lamppost dropped a thin beam of water-milk light. It illuminated a small circle around its base weakly. Farther down the street at pavement level I could see a small white cross marking a pedestrian island in Park Lane. Nothing else. Then out of the dark a whining rumble, a headlight no stronger than a bicycle lamp with the battery run down, and a bus swashed by. I could see people inside it.

I stood looking at this city in the dark, my eyes gradually picking out vague silhouettes of buildings and trees in the park. I looked at my watch, which I could see in the dark. It was a few minutes past seven. While I was looking, the siren began.

Lots of people have described the sound of an air-raid siren. It is not as terrifying as you think. Rather—I suppose—the quality of terror depends upon one's own emotional state. The time an air-raid siren really frightened me was when, after an early "all clear," it went off again about two o'clock in the morning, when I was taxiing through deserted streets. Then its rising and falling wail echoing against the empty buildings made me cold all over and I wanted to get the hell out of there, because I knew that in a moment there would be guns going off and bombs would fall and maybe I would achieve a time and space coincidence with one.

The siren, of course, is not one siren, but many. The

sirens are all over town. They do not stop and start all at once. One starts and just as it gets under way another picks up the note. And then another and another until the whole town is echoing. There is no siren very near the Dorchester, which is perhaps why it did not startle me more. Day in, day out the "alerts" and the "all clears" served me principally as reminders that there was a war on.

What with one siren picking up another the wail may continue for several minutes, which is a long time if you're waiting for it to be over to resume a conversation. But indoors you are more apt than not to fail to hear it —which is why in public buildings air-raid wardens stick their heads in, blow police whistles, and shout, and why just inside the revolving door of the Dorchester there is always a big sign three by four feet square which says either AIR-RAID WARNING or ALL CLEAR.

The practice of one siren picking up another was continually confusing to me when it came to the all clear. The all-clear signal is given by the same siren that gives the warning. The difference between the warning signal and the all-clear signal is that during the warning the note rises and falls. I think it's done by simply turning the siren off every time it gets well wound up and then almost immediately starting it again. In the all-clear signal the siren winds up to its top note and stays there. So that when one siren after another picks up the all-clear signal, just after the first siren has arrived at its highest note the second one begins winding up to *its*. So that the confusion sounds quite like an alert.

Just as nobody pays much attention to alarms during the day, nobody pays any mind to all clears during the night—for they are almost certain to be followed presently by another alarm.

That first evening in the Dorchester, the siren was no more than a curiosity to me. I was interested to be hearing the real thing at last, surprised only that it was not louder and more ominous than it was.

About five minutes later the raid began. There is a good deal of debate in the papers about when the government should sound the alarm—that is, how long before the raiders will arrive over the city. The raiders, of course, have been followed up from the Channel, and the central bureau knows where each enemy ship or squadron is, which way it is coming, and how fast. Some people who write to the papers seem to think the timing of the alarm does not give them enough minutes to find and get into a shelter.

The first attack I watched out the bathroom window, like the air-raid warning I heard, was more of a curiosity and a spectacle than either a dramatic or a sobering experience.

First there was the thud of a gun over the horizon, then another and another. When the clouds are low the crash of the guns echoes into a rumble that is exactly like thunder, far off and continuous. But on a clear night such as my first, the discharge of each gun is individual and distinct. Ten seconds after the first guns went off over the horizon, batteries on the edge of the city picked up the refrain. I recognized another caliber cannon that fired very rapidly, five or six shots. Pup, pup, pup, pup, pup. A hollow sound. I found Ben Robertson next to me at the window. He said, "That's a Bofors. It's a Swedish gun. The Germans use it too." Then against the skyline a white flash, fan-shaped. Ben thought it was a naval gun. "There's one in the park right in front of us." I looked into the dark and thought of a crew such as I'd seen by daylight on the way from the coast, standing rigidly about their gun, their helmeted heads thrown back, motionless, watching the sky. I thought: "They wouldn't be doing that at night." I said, "How do they aim at night?" Ben said, "People say by guess and by God."

Suddenly first one and two, then three, four, five searchlights went on along the edge of the city from whence the firing came. They shot straight up. Hard fountains of light that seemed to dissolve into infinity. Ben said he thought they reached 20,000 feet, which is four miles, or eighty New York block lengths. I watched them night after night and never saw them catch a plane. After a few minutes they began to move in awkward arcs. They crossed and recrossed one another. Their light seemed more concentrated than the light of searchlights that play from battleships in the Hudson. They kept feeling around in the sky. Then up near where two of them crossed, tiny fireworks went off, one, two, three, four sharp white flashes.

"Those are the shells of the guns you heard go off a few seconds ago," said Ben. "How long ago?" I asked him. "Ten to fourteen seconds," he said. "When a gun goes off near you you can count and look up and see the explosion of the shell."

More searchlights went on, more guns went off. But all some miles away. I was leaning on my elbows on the window sill. Then suddenly from right overhead the noise of the motors came down. The noise of the motors of an enemy plane over your head is what stops an air raid seeming just a spectacle. The noise of the motors scared me.

In New York I live directly under the beam on which planes travel west from LaGuardia Field. Douglas D.C. 3's with two 1000-horsepower motors pass and repass all day and all night. The sound of a twin-motor German bomber 20,000 feet in the air over London does not sound at all like the roar of the Douglas climbing out of LaGuardia toward the Alleghenies. The note is pitched higher and has almost a whine in it. There is an uneven cadence to it. This is the result of the two motors being out of synchronization. The pilots of twin-motor commercial planes adjust their propeller revolutions until the motors synchronize and the note you hear is even and constant. The pilots of bombers over enemy territory throw their motors out of step in order to make it harder for sound-wave-catching devices to locate them.*

Ed Murrow says the German bombers over London hum a nasal refrain which goes, "Where are *you?* Where are *you?* Where are *you?*" The sound is definitely unfriendly. Like the searchlights, the planes too seem to be searching. They *are* searching. They go back and forth and round and round. As you look up into nothing and hear them you may think, "There is a man sitting and in his hand is a push button on the end of a wire—like the button hanging down over the back of your bed in a hotel. And when he presses that button the steel fingers that hold the bomb in the belly of his flying machine relax and the bomb drops. He could squeeze the button now. Or now. Or now. And on when he squeezes will depend whether the bomb that falls will land five miles that way, five miles the other way, or come down through the roof over my head."

This is all fantasy because, as I shall presently explain, most of the bombs dropped over London are probably released automatically by wireless control dictated in the *Luftwaffe* headquarters. But once you've seen the innocent-looking little button the bombers have to press to release their loads you cannot get out of your head the whimsicality of the dropping of death and destruction from the air.

The German motors over my head moved away. Sud-

* The experienced can tell when a German bomber pilot gets the wind up by the sound of his motors. When antiaircraft fire gets hot around him he is liable to open both throttles wide to get more power and speed and thus throw his motors back in synchronization.

denly the gun in Hyde Park went off. It went off so suddenly and violently it almost literally threw me back
from the window. The conception of a gun crash split-
ting the air is inadequate. It seems to fractionalize it.
The curtains and I blew back together. Out of the center
of the all-enveloping noise came a high, thin whine, fad-
ing rapidly. A whine with a swoosh in it. When I first
heard it I only knew it was there. Later I came to recog-
nize it as the whistle of the shell going up. I knew the
crash was a gun and it did not frighten me. I leaned back
out the window and started to count to see if I could tell
when the shell was to explode. It came, a sharp white
flash, this time not where I was looking in the dark, but
off to the right. And then a second later the noise of the
shell bursting, a hollow thump like someone knocking
gently on heaven. The explosion of the shell released
something in me. I suddenly felt very angry at the plane
over London and very good about the bursting shell. I
wanted the gun below me to shoot again and again. I
wanted it to reach up and slap that bastard down. The
plane had come up from the south, crossed overhead,
and was proceeding north. The guns on the other side
of London began to shoot at it. I found I was so anxious
that they'd hit it that I was leaning out the window pant-
ing.

Every once in a while when I was in London that feeling would come back to me. And in bed, half asleep, the
dull thuds and crashes of the antiaircraft guns would be
comforting to me. These guns were on my side. They
were shooting at people who were trying to kill me and
whom I didn't like. This is what people mean, I suppose,
when they say that half the importance of antiaircraft
fire in a city is its good effect on the morale of the inhabitants.

The noise of the guns does not always work this way. I
have come home to the Dorchester tired and cold and

had the gun outside the window make me jump and hate it every time it went off. It has made me want to get down and crawl in the cellar where I wouldn't hear it. But when you hear the German first and then the gun shooting at him, that's a fine sensation.

On the first evening, after that one plane had passed right above me the show was over. I do not know where he dropped his bombs. I neither saw nor heard them fall. The guns died away, the searchlights went out. I could hear a policeman walking on the street below. Another bus passed.

The German planes did not come back until we were at dinner.

REQUIEM FOR
A LOST SOCIETY

I TALK A LOT about the Dorchester Hotel. Not simply because I stayed there but because it really is a unique place in London, a unique and curious place in the world. I would give a good deal to be really sure just how significant it is—to be *sure* for instance that it is utterly insignificant.

I have written about the Dorchester by day—its normalcy—and about the Dorchester in the middle of the night, with people tucked away in the corners asleep. Neither of these phenomena is confusing. What's confusing is the Dorchester at dinner. I dined there the first night after watching my first air raid from my bathroom window, with the Duff Coopers and a gay and pleasant group including Eve Curie, daughter of the great scientists, in London, working and writing against the Vichy government. We dined in the room in which they dance and we talked a lot about it. Every time I went in there —with American journalists, with English journalists, with officers in the Army and the Air Force, with politicians and friends, we talked about the room at the Dorchester in which they danced at dinnertime. After you have been there several times it gets boring because it's always exactly the same. But still you talk about it because it's so patently difficult to understand.

It's a ghost of a room in which people danced and drank in 1917 and '18. It's peopled with French officers and Polish officers, Englishmen in gay guards uniforms, young Americans from the Eagle Squadron, which is the walking ghost of the Lafayette Squadron from Paris. The girls the officers have with them are very beautiful—very —and are beautifully and immaculately dressed, with their hair exceedingly well waved. I don't remember whether girls polished their nails in 1918 but if they had thought of it they would have. It is peopled with very cosmopolitan people. A Negress and a distinguished-looking Englishman. A handsome young lady smoking a cigar. Monocles are in female as well as male eyes. Men who are not in uniform are not dressed. (This, I suppose, is an important news note: the Englishman no longer dresses for dinner in London. The only dinner clothes I saw worn in England were by two men who looked like traveling salesmen in a hotel in a provincial town.)

There is a jazz band to play for this company and a number of the dancers have had too much to drink. The color of the faces is high and the note of the conversation slightly hysterical. Many are drinking champagne.

"Those who are about to die" must raise the glass once more. One last fling before the leave expires. That is the way it was in 1918. And here are these people acting out the same part. Only the point is, with the exception of the occasional young aviator sitting looking at it all in some bewilderment, these people are not about to die. They are not on leave from the trenches in Flanders. They are officers and citizens of a country that is engaged in a very different kind of war from the war that lasted from 1914 to '18. What is about to expire is not the breath in their bodies but their property rights in banks and mortgages. What is about to end is life as they knew and lived it as "the international set"—the people who are always in Biarritz and Cannes at the right time of year in the right hotels.

While they danced the guns outside shook the building and overhead the Dorniers droned back and forth, back and forth. And every bomb the Dorniers dropped might destroy some property they owned and every shell the antiaircraft raised might be paid for by their taxes.

How many of those who were there were spectators like myself and the young aviators and how many were really engaged in desperate make-believe that this war was like the last and that when it was won they would go back to their bars and their beaches wherever the weather was pleasantest in Europe I have no way of knowing.

But the make-believe part of it was inescapable. One had the strongest feeling that the band was about to stop, the drums to roll, and then would come Irene Castle to dance. Or Elsie Janis to sing to the boys who were about to die. It was an overdone movie, beautifully costumed but badly directed by a man who had made B movies all his life.

I talked to a lot of people in London about the Dorchester at dinnertime and never found one who knew it who wasn't in some subtle and yet obvious way ashamed of it. There is too much reality in London for make-believe. This is not a war of gay guards uniforms and jazz bands and pretty girls in frocks that cost £50. And nobody in London who had anything to do with the war —from air-raid wardens to Cabinet ministers—even holdovers from the then-dying Mr. Chamberlain's Cabinet— appeared to be under any illusion about the fact. Yet there was the Dorchester dancing away—and a few other hotels, diluted solutions of the Dorchester.

The first night when I dined there it made me laugh.

And I kept saying, "But this isn't so." And people at the table with me laughed too and said, "You're quite right. It isn't." Someone said, "Wouldn't it be wonderful if a bomb came in now? It would be like watching the *Titanic* sink over again." The *Titanic* was the boat that hit the iceberg and went down with all the fashionables sitting on the decks, smoking and making jokes while the band played, and the boat sank and drowned them all. Then somebody said, "But why shouldn't they come here and dance? What else should they do? Most of those girls drive ambulances or run canteens or help someplace. Why shouldn't they get dressed up and come here and dance? Even if it isn't their war any more."

Nobody could think why they shouldn't. Still everyone knew that they didn't belong in London in 1940. Everyone knew and they knew. Outside the big gun crashed again. And the glasses shook on the table. Someone said, "That dreadful gun."

Then we began to talk about Egypt.

After dinner Ben Robertson and I went to find Ed Murrow, who lives in a pleasant flat not far from the broadcasting building. We sat and talked for an hour. He told us about the young English bomber pilot who had sat where I was sitting while waiting to broadcast about a flight over Berlin. A stick of bombs had come down across the street. They'd come whistling, made one, two, three terrific explosions. The bomber had said, "My God! What's that?" Ed had told him they were bombs. He said the pilot was white as a sheet. The bomber pilot shook his head, "I had no idea they were like that."

Murrow told me he had never seen anything like the way the English people took it and praised their cheerfulness and complete confidence. They could take it and come back to win. He said he doubted if there ever had been anything like it. He said, "The English will drive you crazy. They are so slow. It takes them so long to get around to doing anything."

But he said, "They do get around to it. I get worried about them. But they get around to it."

Because I urged him, he told me about narrow escapes he had had. Several times he had been knocked down on the street, and houses around him had been blown down. He told me funny stories about how a friend had just come to town and was sitting in the apartment and he was describing the noises in London and saying, "An incendiary bomb goes like this: swish-swosh and then a plunk. And then another swish-swosh and another plunk." And then as if in echo came the sounds, "Swish-swosh, swish-swosh, swish-swosh, plunk, plunk, plunk." And there were incendiary bombs on the roof upstairs. They went up and put them out with shovelfuls of sand.

He told about the time the broadcasting studio was full of sleeping people and he tried to keep his voice down so as not to wake them. And New York had cabled the next day asking what was the matter. Had it all got too much for him? He'd sounded as if he was sobbing.

He told about the time he risked his neck with a young technician named Kenneth Matthews in the Ministry of Information to record the whistles and explosions of bombs with a sound-truck recording apparatus and how when he wanted to put them on the air he was told off from the home office—it was "against Columbia's policy to play records." And how he put them on anyway. I told him I had heard the broadcast and that I wanted to bring the records back with me. And later I arranged this. By a coincidence I had a letter to Matthews from a mutual friend and he got me the records and I have them. They are very effective. Especially when played in the dark.

He told me what he thought about a lot of individuals —bad, indifferent, and good. How he felt about different phases of the war. He said that just for fun he asked his home office to make inquiries on whether the Germans would let him come to Berlin to broadcast and how he got back this extraordinary answer: "We will be very glad to have Mr. Murrow represent Columbia Broadcasting Company in Berlin, providing he is willing to give us his word as a gentleman that after coming to Berlin he will not visit England again until after the war."

About midnight we went out and drove around to the broadcasting building. Ben Robertson has a taxi driver named Calligan, always so called, who will go anywhere any time. Mr. Calligan calls himself and his cab "The Never-Fail Taxi Co." He said he likes to drive at night because he thinks it safer. Less chance to be hit moving about. Before the war Mr. Calligan called himself and his cab "The Spooners Special Taxi Cab Company."

Going down to broadcast to America is an experience. The transmitters, of course, are a long way off, but the control rooms in the studios of the BBC building are obviously of military importance. When the Fascist coups first began it was always the central broadcasting station plotters planned to take. The BBC headquarters are better guarded than 10 Downing Street. The building itself is enormous, modern, a landmark and a target for bombers. It has been hit only once, with a medium-sized time bomb that came sliding in a window six or seven stories up. It went through one floor, slithered along the next, and lay still. About the time they got a rope around it it went off. The damage was not great. There is scaffolding on the outside of the building where they are repairing it.

So far in London there is little time or energy left to repair damage to buildings that have been rendered un-inhabitable. Even if only all the windows are broken and perhaps the roof cracked it is simply abandoned. But the damage to the BBC building is so slight it is being fixed.

The entryway is heavily sandbagged and just inside stands a sentry with a rifle and bayonet. He has a steel bell sentry box. The office building like the foyer is cut in two with heavy iron screening. And there are more guards at the door through the screening. Even Ed Murrow could not take us through this gateway until we had gone to a window and registered our particulars. Then we went through the screen across the foyer and down three long flights of stairs. At the foot of each was a gas door—like a waterproof compartment door in an ocean liner.

On the floor of each basement we passed through there were men sleeping. This was my first sight of the most characteristic phenomenon of the basements of all kinds of buildings in London by night. Hotels, offices, newspaper buildings, warehouses, private houses: sleeping people. In blankets, on mattresses. Sitting propped up in corners, on bunks, on boxes, under stairways. On their backs, on their sides, curled up hugging things like children. With their feet in each others' faces. Men and women. Women and men and children. Not so many children. But often children. Sleeping in the dark. Sleeping in dim light. Sleeping with bright, blazing light shining down on their faces. Sleeping soundlessly. Sleeping noisily. Sometimes opening one eye to look up.

Down in the BBC building, past gas locks and sleeping figures and, on the lower floors, past more sentries. Here I saw my first guardsmen in the primitive—men in mufti with arm bands, sitting with loaded shotguns across their knees. Ed Murrow joked with one of them and said, "I'm always afraid one of you fellows is going to take a shot at me some night." The nearest guardsman said, "I am. You don't know how much I want to shoot this thing off."

The broadcasting studio from which the international news goes out is a small room not over ten by twenty divided in the middle by a curtain. In the half you come into there are a typewriter and a sofa littered with stuff. Beyond the curtain is a little green beige-covered table on which a microphone stands, brightly lit by a hanging bell-shaded light. On either side of the table are kitchen chairs. Beyond in the corner is another little table where a very bored man sits playing with a pencil. He's one of the censors.

Ed Murrow either brings the script with him or sits down at the typewriter and writes it. Then he gives it to the censor, who reads it and passes it back.

All three American chains broadcast from this room, Fred Bate for the National Broadcasting Company, Arthur Mann for the Mutual. Mann does not broadcast as often as the other two, for the WOR people rely more on Raymond Gram Swing to do their foreign-news analyzing in New York. Later in my stay I broadcast once with Ed Murrow and once with Mann. I brought my script to the censor. He made no comment. I never knew whether he approved or disapproved, but he passed it anyway. It is the broadcaster's privilege to argue with the censor. If the argument gets hot, one of them calls up the Ministry of Information and appeals to a higher authority. The argument sometimes gets hot. Ed said not often.

The ritual of the international broadcast is simple in extreme. There is the broadcasting studio's usual clock with a large second hand on the wall. Murrow talks first at 12:45—in the middle of the night—the broadcast we hear at 6:45 in the evening. By 12:35 he had finished his piece and at 12:40 the censor had read it. I sat down across the table from him and he handed me a set of earphones. He said, "You will hear some of the program ahead of me in the earphones. Then we talk for a minute or two with the studio in New York on the carrier wave. We check how much time I have. Usually that is easy, unless they are picking up some other foreign capital blind. Then it is hard to fit together."

Presently the earphones began to tell me about something that was being advertised in the U. S. I forget what. Then it was switched on to the carrier wave and Ed began talking with Paul White who is in charge of special programs in the Columbia office in New York. I knew White a long time ago and recognized his voice. He was very cheerful, spoke loudly and distinctly. Said something like, "Well, what are you up to tonight, Ed?" Ed said he was going to be as brilliant as always and there was some laughter back and forth. Ed said, "I have Ralph Ingersoll here in the office"; and then across the table to me, "Would you like them to call up anyone for you?" I said yes. "Ask them to call my office and tell them the Germans missed me by a mile." I told them the number was STerling 3-2501. The rest of the carrier wave was used trying to get this information to America because White, who knew I had a house near Salisbury, Connecticut, insisted the number must be Salisbury 3-2501. I didn't feel we got this straightened out. The conversation closed with a brisk "so long." The carrier wave was switched off. The second hand on the clock showed ten seconds left. They passed in silence and then Ed Murrow began talking so smoothly that I could not believe he was reading from the copy that lay on the table in front of him.

When he was through he told me about the night the bomb came into the BBC building. It went off not long before he was to go on the air, and just as he began talking they carried two friends of his past the studio on stretchers. They'd taken them from the first-aid hospital down the hall in the basement. They were dead.

We said good night to the censor and went up past the home guard with the loaded shotgun, through the gas locks and over the feet of sleeping men and women.

We stopped and peeked into the great BBC concert hall. This was really the first big shelter I saw. The seats were out of it and the whole floor and the whole stage were carpeted solid with human figures. It was almost dark in the hall and it took a minute to grasp the scene and understand it. Ed said, "The people are in their first sleep and that's why they are so quiet." Later on in the night he said they would be more restless and there would be coughing and turning.

It's a strange feeling to be standing in the doorway and looking into a concert hall in which people are not listening to a concert but sleeping on the floor en masse. My first surprise was at how tight they were packed. Later on I got used to this. In all but the swankiest and daintiest shelters in London people sleep packed tightly. Face against face. Buttocks against buttocks. Elbows overlapping.

After a while, when my eyes got used to it, I could identify family groups—father, mother, child, curved into one another like piled saucers set on edge. As I remember, everyone in the concert-hall shelter was prostrate. More typical is it to see at least a few people propped upright in one chair or in two, with their legs on the second, or semireclining in canvas deck chairs. Everyone in the concert hall seemed to have a mattress to lie on. The people were not undressed. You could see that from parts of them that were uncovered. The air was good.

When we got up on to the streets I told Ed I was interested in shelters and the next night planned to do the rounds. He said, "Let's see what we find around here."

Besides a few shaded street lamps, traffic signals, and the little crosses marking obstructions, the only other lighted objects on the streets of London are the dimly illuminated signs which read simply ARP, with an arrow underneath. ARP means Air-Raid Protection and the arrows point to the nearest shelter. Everywhere you go all over England you see these signs. I told Ben Robertson he should write a piece about the lost land of Arp, for everywhere you went there were signs directing the traffic to it. But you could walk the streets forever without finding it.

The lost land of Arp is underground. We found our entrance to it—dimly shaded light reflecting on a cellar doorway. We pushed the door in, found ourselves in a shadowy hall. We walked along the hall twenty or thirty feet and stopped as it turned a right angle. Just beyond the angle was a tableau, a set piece. Seated opposite each other on two packing boxes were respectively a pretty girl in blue denim overalls and a bearded old man. Between them was a chessboard. Two men stood motionless behind the old man, watching the game. We watched for a full minute until the girl, whose hand was poised, moved a piece, and we shuffled our feet. The girl jumped. "You startled me," she said. Then Ben said, "We are newspaper people and we would like to look around. Might we?" The girl was an air-raid warden in charge of the shelter. She was very agreeable. Her shelter was a small one in the basement of a private house, I gathered. Each of half a dozen cellar rooms that opened off the hall were like the concert hall—carpeted with sleeping people. There was nothing remarkable about them except that it continued to seem odd to me to see floors packed solid with people wrapped in blankets. We talked with the girl about how many people were there and who they were and whether the same people came back every night and when. I have seen so many shelters since that I have forgotten the details of that one. She thought it was characteristic of the shelters in that neighborhood. It was dry, cool, and the air was good. Its toilet facilities were limited and every square inch of sleeping space seemed used, but there were no people propped in the halls or on the stairs. There were no extra rooms for recreation. Everything was very quiet.

When the young lady found out I had come from America she became very interested and told me that if I would come back the next night she would arrange for someone to look after her shelter and take me around to others. We had no special credentials. Nowhere that I went in underground London at night did I ever present credentials or was I ever met with anything but simple courtesy and friendliness. Nor did any shelter warden I met hesitate in answering questions or showing me about. To a man and woman they seemed so genuinely interested in their jobs, so "keen" is the English word, that they were quickly responsive to my interests.

We left the young lady to play chess with the old man and went up on to the street again. It was after two o'clock. Far away the guns were going again. I could not hear the planes. We went back to Ed Murrow's flat and drank and talked for another hour. It was after three when I got back to the hotel. I said to Ben, "Why not spend the rest of the night here with me? There are twin beds." We were both very tired and he stayed. There was some talk later about my sleeping in my bed on the seventh floor of the Dorchester. I was credited with having made a decision to sleep aboveground while I was in London. I don't ever remember having made such a decision. I was exactly that naïve when I came to London that it never occurred to me that a decision on where to sleep was called for. I was just so damn tired when I got back to the hotel at the end of my first full day in England that I would have slept sitting up on a curbstone if someone had said decisively, "There is where you are to sleep."

No one in London credited me with being brave for sleeping in my bed on the seventh floor. Or for being foolhardy. I simply say that people remarked on the fact that I slept there because everybody in London is interested in where everybody else sleeps and it is fairly standard to remark during a preliminary conversation with people you meet or fall into conversation with, "Where do you sleep?" There is no pressure of society one way or the other. No one is looked down on or looked up to for sleeping any particular place unless it be the Turkish-bath shelter in the Dorchester which is quite another story. But almost everybody except me knew why he or she slept where he did. Each reasoned it out for himself. Those who slept aboveground generally explained that they did not like the idea of a building falling on top of them or that the odds against a direct hit were too great to bother about. Those who slept in shelters often said that quiet was the important thing, that the guns spoiled their sleep.

Relatively few of London's shelters I came to see when I visited them are positive protection against a direct hit from a large bomb. But most of them are certainly safer than sleeping aboveground. They afford protection from either a small bomb or anything but a direct hit from a large one. But certainly if night bombing continues, some packed shelters will be hit during the course of the winter and some groups or hundreds of people buried beneath the buildings under which they crawl to sleep.

But as for me I never made a real decision because when it came time to go to bed the first day I was too tired to care. Not even the six-inch gun disturbed my slumber.

VI

DEATH IN THE DARK

THERE WAS not much pattern to my days in London. The difficulty of making and changing arrangements by telephone and the fact that from the second day till the day before I left I was waiting on my appointment with the Prime Minister—its time and place was not set until an hour before I saw him—meant that I could make no commitments in advance. Each day I simply made and kept as many engagements as I was able. Ben Robertson, who slept with me the first night, simply stayed on.

I have had difficulty since I got back making people really understand how entirely casually people take sleeping anywhere they happen to be when the blackout comes in London. Possibly it's because the phrase sleeping with someone has connotations in our vocabulary. Possibly it's because the idea of not having a room of one's own to sleep in every night is so foreign to everyone's experience here.

I asked everyone I met in and out of the government how many Londoners slept in shelters and how many slept in their homes. No one had any idea. There are no statistics whatever available. Estimates of the number who slept in shelters, public and private, varied from fifty per cent to ninety-five per cent. The only thing you can be sure of is that very few sleep normally, night after night, in their own beds in their own rooms. Households who do not take to shelters go down to the hall downstairs, or into the cellar. In hotels you find people sleeping in the halls—presumably to get away from the noise and the possibility of flying glass from the windows.

Even leaving out the fear of being out during heavy raiding you must also realize the difficulty of moving about a complicated city like London during a blackout. There are taxis that cruise all night, but they are few. Few also are the busses and the trains and the tubes. It was, for instance, altogether natural that, when I had a radio talk to dictate during my second week and a young lady public stenographer came to type it for me and the work went on without either of us noticing the time until suddenly the maid came in and drew the curtains for the blackout, Ben and I should offer her our couch to sleep on. And she should debate for some minutes before deciding her roommate might be worried and she didn't mind taking the bus anyway. A house lent to a young officer friend of mine by his aunt never had less than a dozen inhabitants a night, and never the same dozen.

You must realize what it does to convention to take in first relatives, then acquaintances and finally strangers who were bombed out. And you must also realize—perhaps the most important thing of all—that when the night is full of noise no one wants to be alone. The presence of other human beings is comforting.

I think the only time I was really all out frightened— literally panicked—was when I came in alone one late afternoon and Ben, who was to join me, did not show up for several hours. It was the night a new and still larger gun moved into the park opposite. I was told it was a six-inch navy gun. It began to go off right after the first alarm. I went to watch from my bathroom-dark-room. There was a storm over London and the wind howled through the open window. Shells from the gun burst directly overhead, so that I ducked each time, sure the shrapnel would fall where I was. If it did, I heard none of it. But the crash of the gun was first deafening and then suddenly terrifying. I bolted the window and went in and tried to read the evening paper. The gun kept crashing and crashing and crashing. All of a sudden it came—a terrific desire to get to some other place in a hurry. I went out and rang for the elevator. It was about 8:30.

As I got in, a very elegant old dame came down the corridor and got in with me. The gun went off. She said, "What was that?" A freckled elevator man said, "That was me, ma'am." She said, "Well, I wish to heaven you'd told me it was you. You've been scaring the life out of me." When I got down to the lobby people were standing around talking and going into dinner quite normally. I knew what I wanted to do. I wanted to go down into the boiler room, get into a corner and curl up where I couldn't hear that damn gun. I thought if I did, when Ben came in he would be ashamed of me. I said nuts to myself. The gun went off a couple of times more and shook the revolving door. It made the sign reading AIR-RAID WARNING flap. I said to myself, "Look here. You've decided that if you're going to be hit you're going to be hit. If you play it any other way you're sure to lose. Like changing your stake gambling." I said to myself, "You may be scared, but you know very well that the odds of a bomb hitting you are approximately seven or eight million to one." I went back upstairs and felt much better. Presently Ben came in with Helen Kirkpatrick of *The Chicago Daily News*. They had been talking to somebody.

The point about being afraid during a bombardment in which you know the chances of being killed are minute is this: after you've been frightened a few times you know that being frightened is just an unreasonable temporary emotion, that it will pass, and that in a little while you will feel all right again. Like getting unreasonably mad at a telephone girl giving you the wrong number. The time when I was alone with the gun noise in the Dorchester was the only time I felt panic, but four or five times in any given night, even though they were relatively quiet, I was scared and each time after a while the fear would pass and I'd feel all right again. Because I was always with people who if they were scared didn't show it and we went about what we decided as our business and everything was all right and the fear passed.

I think it's this quality of keeping their fears to themselves while they are afraid—they talk about it plenty afterwards—that's the most important part of what the English call "behaving well." They have it whether they are cockneys in the East End or Cabinet ministers. They do not transmit their fears to one another the way some other peoples do. And when people transmit their fears to each other the result is panic and anything can happen in a panic. When they don't transmit their fear they go on about their business and presently aren't afraid any more.

I talked this over with a number of people in London and they agreed with me.

The fear that I'm talking about is the unreasonable fear produced by noise and the imagination. How a soldier who is under fire and is liable to be killed in action feels I know only from books. But I was and am interested in the other kind of fear, because that is the principal tool with which Adolf Hitler has conquered so much of the world. It's the Britisher's ability to cope with it and to survive it and to learn that it's a headache and not a fatal disease that's an important part of my confidence that the British will withstand and survive

Adolf Hitler, and there's absolutely no question that they survived the terrific dose he gave them in September and are flourishing under the dilute solution which seems all he is currently able to administer now.

The two weeks that I was in London were what are called quiet weeks. They are quiet because Hitler has no control over the air of England in the daylight and because night bombers work best in the full of the moon when they can steer and guide their bombs by the reflection of the moon on the water and the rivers and lakes of England. The moon was on the wane when I arrived.

I know what it can be like when the moon is full, because the three days just before I got to London included the worst night bombing of the war so far. So I saw London right after its three worst nights and the people I talked to had just been through these nights.

From the point of view of personal experience I have identified this distinction: the difference between a quiet night and a rough night in London is simply that on a rough night if you move about the city streets you will have at least one narrow escape per night; that is, at least one bomb will whistle down and explode within a half a block or a block of you sometime or other. Whereas, going about on "quiet nights," while there is the same raiding, the guns and the lights and the planes, the bombs they drop are so scattered that in fourteen nights I had only two small bombs drop within a block of me, one in the park outside my window—after learning to sleep through the naval gun, its whistle woke me wide awake just before it hit—and the other on a road along which we were driving back to town from a night flying field. There were four of us in a closed Woolsey car. The gears on the Woolsey were noisy and we had heard no warning, but a red light flashed in front of us and an air-raid warden stuck his head in as we stopped. He said, "There's a crater just ahead. It's just happened.

We haven't found it yet. Better be careful." We said we would and drove on.

At the end of a block we all at once saw two small lights flush with the pavement. The next minute we began to run over rubble. One of us said, "It's right here. You can always tell when you begin running over rubble." Another few feet and we saw what the lights on the street were. They were the still-burning sidelights of a car that had just run into the crater. A woman came toward us out of the black and said, "Where are you going?"

The driver said, "To London."

She said, "No, no, no, I mean what part of London?"

The driver said, "The West End."

Her voice was rising. It sounded hysterical. She said, "No, no, no, that won't do at all. That's not at all where I want to go," and ran off behind us. We think she had been in the car.

We swung off to one side to avoid it and the pencil beam of our headlight picked out a figure lying on the edge of the curb. We got out and went over to it. It was a dead policeman. A redheaded policeman. He had been young and good-looking. There was no one else around. It was very quiet. You could hear water bubbling under the car. The bomb had broken a main. We had flash-lights and stood looking down at the dead policeman, not quite knowing what to do next. Presently there were footsteps coming rapidly toward us. Two air-raid ward-ens. They made no comment. First one and then several policemen came from another street. They looked at the dead policeman, but did not move him. We shifted uneasily and walked back to look in the crater. The bomb must have hit just ahead of the car and the car rolled in where the pavement had been. For it was hardly scratched. While we were looking an ambulance or a truck rolled up behind us, some men got out, went

over to where the warden was standing over the casualty.
They lifted the dead policeman onto the stretcher, carried him back into the darkness. And no one said anything. The ambulance or the morgue wagon or whatever
it was went off into the dark. The wardens and the policemen were in conference over how to get the car out
of the crater. Down the street we could see another
warden bringing a red lantern to mark it.

There had been some joking in the car about my not
having had a close one in ten days in London. One of
the men said, "Well, if it had to happen, I'm glad it
happened where you could see it. This is just routine. I
think there must be a bicycle about. I think the policeman was going home on it when the bomb hit." It was
no longer a joke that I have the experience of having a
bomb go off near me. The face of the dead policeman
with the red hair stayed with me. That and the suddenness with which it happened and the silence that was
around it after it happened. I began to feel anger rising
in me. I stayed acutely angry for several hours at the
people who had killed the policeman. Then, like being
afraid, the acute part passed.

I had picked up a piece of the shell. I found it with
my flashlight imbedded in the pavement and wedged it
out. I brought it home with me.

I started to write about my days in London and fell
to writing about what it feels like to be frightened by
bombs, and how you find while you keep getting frightened you keep getting over it.

When I started I was saying that there was no pattern
to my days except that I saw as many people in the government as I could get hold of and filled in the time between. During the day I filled it in with riding around
London looking at the damage. I went to the railway
stations and the docks and different parts of the city. But

almost every night I spent going from shelter to shelter, talking with wardens and policemen and, depending on the time of night, people who were just coming in to go to bed or who had lain down but had been unable to go to sleep.

The first question that most people asked me when I got back was, "How much is London really damaged?" I can give you a generalization: physically I found it damaged quite a little more than I expected; spiritually a very great deal less. A month or two ago Ben Robertson wrote this generalization: that the damage was spotty; that you could map one route along which the traveler would see no evidence of destruction. And that you could map another along which some building or landmark in every block had been blasted. This generalization of two months ago has to be altered: I was not able to drive half a mile anywhere in London proper without seeing damage.

What I find people in this country unsophisticated about is the vast variety of kinds of damage implied by the word "bombed." Big, little, and negligible. I have looked back at the headlines American papers carried about damage I have seen with my own eyes in London and almost always been surprised how misleading the headline was despite its literal accuracy. For example, take the accurate headline BUCKINGHAM PALACE BOMBED. What kind of picture did newspaper readers gets from such a headline? Probably the total destruction of Buckingham Palace. Actually, it was hit with a small bomb. It was not destroyed at all. I did not go into it, but it doesn't look as if it were rendered uninhabitable or, in the accurate sense of the word, that its inhabitants were "bombed out."

To say a building was hit by a bomb or bombed is an almost meaningless description. It might mean that a few tiles on its roof were broken by a small incendiary. It might mean it had been utterly and completely demolished, violently made not to exist. There is every variation in between. As I said before, total demolition is rare.

To understand bombing and bomb damage you must have a little sophistication about bombs.

There are these kinds of bombs being dropped in London: incendiaries—by the handful, scores, and hundreds. Incendiary bombs have aluminum heads two and a half inches in diameter. They contain a chemical that burns with an intense heat—2500 degrees Fahrenheit, I am told —the minute they hit. But they are so easy to put out that the fire department's rarely called for them. If you can reach them within a few minutes, a small shovelful of sand will extinguish them. All the roofs in London have sand handy. Every roof is watched by spotters on it or on other roofs. These small incendiary bombs do not cause much damage and are sneeringly regarded in London.

Oil bombs are cylindrical oil drums. Some say they are filled with crankcase drainings, and some say with a special oil so sluggish it will hardly flow until ignited and then flows rapidly and spreads as its temperature rises. Whatever is inside it, it is an extremely unpopular guest. But it does no harm unless it falls on some dwelling that is inflammable.

The high-explosive bombs come in four sizes, roughly 100-pound, 250-, 500-, and 1000-pound. The smaller are much commoner than the bigger. They often drop in what are called sticks—three at a time, striking along a straight line, perhaps 100 yards apart. The smaller ones will render an ordinary dwelling uninhabitable, but have not the force to demolish.

All of these bombs come down at an angle, from no matter how high they are dropped. But when they are dropped from very high the angle is almost vertical and if they hit the roof they tend to go down through a building and explode in the basement. This guts the building, renders it uninhabitable. It usually breaks all the windows in adjoining houses and across the street. But these may be replaced or boarded up.

The smallest of these bombs, hitting on a field or on a pavement, makes a crater perhaps ten feet across and six or eight feet deep. Don't hold me to accurate measurements, but these are not far off. I have seen bigger craters, up to twenty or thirty feet in diameter and ten to fifteen feet deep.

All these sizes of bombs are fitted with one of two kinds of fuses: fuses which cause them to explode on or very shortly after contact, and time fuses. Bombs with time fuses are called time bombs. Because they do not explode on contact they are apt to penetrate farther either into the ground or into a building. There they lie, while the mechanism which will presently explode them does its work. Londoners use this formula: a time bomb is not proved to be a dud until it has failed to explode ninety-six hours after contact. And maybe not then. The delayed explosion is apparently achieved by one of two methods: clockwork or chemicals. In the chemical kind the contact releases acid which eats through metal and finally causes the explosion.

There seem to be no ultimate techniques on diagnosing time bombs, but one method is said to be listening to it with a stethoscope. This is not recommended for amateurs, as whether you hear a dripping or a ticking inside, you are still not informed on when the explosion may be expected. When a time bomb falls, the inhabitants of the house move out, the neighborhood is cleared, the streets roped off. The suicide squad of time-bomb removers about whom so much as been written then goes to work. London is full of tales of them—of their walking through streets with time bombs on their shoulders, of the crew that put one in the back of a taxi and it blew up while they were stopping for a traffic light, of the number they have safely removed and allowed to explode harmlessly in the country, of the number they have rendered harmless by removing the detonating apparatus.

The largest of these bombs, the 500- and 1000-pounders, straight or time, can demolish a small building, make a nasty dent in a big one; but destruction so terrific that people take strangers to show it to them is only accomplished with what Londoners call a land mine.

I could not find out the derivation of the name or whether it was true that they were exploded magnetically, by coming near any piece of metal. But this is true about them: they are ten inches in diameter and nine or ten feet long, weigh better than a ton, and are dropped with parachutes attached. Coming down by parachute they come silently and inaccurately—there is no bomb sight that can aim a drifting parachute. They explode on contact. Their first characteristic is that they make practically no crater, that is, their crater is relatively shallow —three or four feet—in comparison with the damage they do horizontally.

I can best illustrate it to you by describing the effect of a land mine that fell almost in the center of a street crossing. The four houses on the four corners, each five stories high, were demolished, flattened to the ground, obliterated, without being touched by the mine. The four blocks surrounding the four demolished houses were rendered uninhabitable. The twelve blocks surrounding the four blocks that were rendered uninhabitable, surrounding the four houses that were demolished, all witnessed the explosion with broken glass.

There is one place in the East End where the flimsy wooden houses are two stories high, joined in solid blocks. A land mine hitting in their midst is said to have rendered a total of 1200 houses uninhabitable. I did not count the houses, but I saw the place where this mine exploded and I walked several blocks in each direction. There was not a window whole. The uninhabitable houses were beginning to be inhabited again by people returning to them and boarding up their windows and camping out inside.

When I visited the English bomber command it was explained to me that German bombs and English bombs have opposite techniques of destruction. The English bombs have heavy shell casings and aim to damage whatever they hit only partially by concussion and principally by the force of flying fragments. The German bombs are thin-shelled and aim to destroy almost entirely by concussion. The land mine, of course, is a stellar exhibit.

So, to get back to the subject of how seriously is London destroyed, it is now scarred from one end to another. There is no district that has not been hit. Damage from any one bomb varies from broken windows to demolition.

I saw a map, ten by ten feet square, marked with pinheads to show damage to London. I was allowed to look at it for several minutes. This is what I saw:

Along the winding river where the docks and warehouses are—evidence of heavy continuous bombing. Around certain military objectives such as power stations, terminals—concentrated bombing. Two scores for those who believe German bombs seek military objectives.

Over the rest of the area of the city of London, bombs scattered with an almost scientific evenness. The map looked as if whoever stuck the pins in it wanted to be sure that there was no square inch without at least one—positive proof that a major theme of German bombing is nonmilitary in objective, aimed solely at terrifying the civilian population.

As to the accuracy of the bombing of military objectives, here I make no qualifications. The aim is surprisingly, astonishingly, amazingly inaccurate. If a power station is a bull's eye—and it is—for two months the Germans have been shooting at it every single night and peppered and plastered all the target rings around the bull's eye without hitting it. Battersea Power Station stands perhaps the single most impressive landmark on the London skyline. It towers like a gargantuan barn over the river, and above the barn rise three enormous smokestacks. They are huge. They are so huge and the whole business so conspicuous that you would think the most novice of bombers could not fail to hit it. Yet in two months of bombing it has been hit only once and that hit was a nick. Black smoke still pours from its chimneys.

The bridges over the Thames are obvious targets. So obvious that the British have already installed the frameworks of temporary wooden bridges to carry their traffic when and as they are hit. Yet not a single bridge in London has been hit a single time.

I regret to acknowledge that two months ago in an otherwise accurate article on damage in London *PM* printed information it had received that Paddington Station had been destroyed. I took a train out of Paddington Station when I left London. It has a famous glass ceiling. The sooty panes were all intact, the station completely unscarred. And so all over London as I went from military objective to military objective I found again and again the same pattern: the surrounding neighborhood plastered; the military objective untouched or only nicked.

This does not hold for the docks, which were set on fire in September. The burned warehouses are empty and conspicuous. But I stood on the docks in the East End and watched a row of ships being unloaded by cranes with busy switching locomotives running back and forth along the edge of the river.

I am, as a result of what I've seen in London, extremely skeptical about all claims of severe damage to military objectives small in area.

Yet in Holland and Belgium and France there is no doubt whatever that military objectives were utterly demolished—even military objectives as small as country crossroads. The secret of the difference, of course, lies in control of the air. An army that has control of the air—real control of the air, ability to do what it likes in the air—can destroy anything aboveground utterly and completely. An army that has not control of the air, but can only fly into it on a hit-and-run basis or by night and at great altitudes even then, cannot destroy what it likes, must waste its energies and its ammunition in fantastic proportion.

There are possibly around two million individual structures in Greater London, which covers 693 square miles. From 1918 to 1938 a total of 771,759 buildings were put up in London. Unless and until interception by night is effected the Germans can destroy some of those dwellings whenever they care to fly over the city. But it's been figured out that at the rate they are currently destroying them it would take years to demolish London.

The physical damage to civilian London, to sum up, was more general and more extensive than I had imagined. The damage to military targets much less. If you love London the damage you can see there now will make you very sad. The wanton, haphazard ruin. And if it is to go on for a year, as the Londoners themselves expect it to go on while they gain the strength to fight back, it may well become appalling. But at the same time you must remember that all the damage that has been done to date has cost the lives of not more than five or six thousand in the worst month out of 8,000,000 Londoners. And before the year is out the shelters will be stronger and safer. There is no reason to believe that London cannot take it if it continues to want to, and it certainly was prepared to when I was there.

VII

THE PLUMBER IS A LITTLE MAN

ALMOST everyone who inquires about my trip to London asks, "What are the shelters like?"

There is no easy answer, for the question itself is too broad.

It's like asking, "What are living quarters in New York like?" and expecting an answer that will cover Mulberry Street, Park Avenue, Forest Hills, and the Bronx.

There are all kinds of shelters in London—street shelters for passing pedestrians, one-family Anderson shelters, big caves sleeping from one to ten thousand people a night, and medium-sized ones into which a few hundred men and women retire in comparative comfort and convenience.

They come warm and cold, drafty and close, dry and damp, crowded and roomy.

Relatively few are really safe—if you define "safe" as "able to withstand a direct hit from a large bomb." Therefore most are what's technically known as "shallow shelter," as distinct from either "deep" or "surface shelter."

Men, women, and children sleep in them together, clothed. They are lit dimly and policed. Shelter wardens are in charge.

Herbert Morrison's Ministry for Home Security has the responsibility for providing and improving shelters.

The shelter situation is in the midst of a process of improvement, stimulated from below as well as above. Conditions have already improved enormously and, in the two weeks I was in London, I saw evidence of further improvement with my own eyes. But the problem is enormous and very complex.

"What are the shelters in London like?" Rather than attempt a single answer I will try to take you with me on a trip through the worst—and the best—and, finally, the in-between ones, so that you may see and feel them as I, another American, saw and felt them.

On my second night in London I began visiting shelters in earnest. Little Hilde Marchant, the shelter reporter on the *Daily Express,* came to dinner with Ben Robertson and me, and after dinner the *Express* sent its all-night car and we put on our tin helmets and started out.

Tin helmets are hard to get in London. It is commonly agreed that one should wear one at night when the barrage is firing, because shell fragments—commonly miscalled shrapnel—may fall anywhere. None that I was aware of ever fell near me, but I was always apprehensive when I found myself out at night without a helmet, always felt much braver when I had my helmet on.

Douglas Williams, of the Ministry of Information, lent me his while I was in London.* The word "tin" is deceptive, because it sounds light. A tin hat is heavier than anything you have ever worn on your head as a civilian. It's made of thin steel and inside there is a heavy head-

---

* Ben Robertson also brought gas masks for us both, but we never carried them. People carrying gas masks now are the exception rather than the rule, although a number of business houses and government services require employees to bring their gas masks to work. And in the army it is felt that it is only a matter of time before the Germans, frustrated in their bombing, begin to use gas.

band suspended from the steel, so that when you wear it the stiff band circles your head and holds the helmet a fraction of an inch away from your scalp. It has a chin band which you're supposed to put on so that concussion or being knocked or throwing yourself down does not remove the steel pancake. Service steel helmets are khaki-colored and apt to have the top surface sanded. Air-raid wardens' are painted blue with initials A.R.W. in white. Hilde's was black and looked somewhat feminine, but was just as heavy. After you've worn one for some time, if you're not used to it, it gives you a headache. But we kept them on in shelters because we decided they made us look less like slummers and more like officials.

Hilde, whose mind is always made up, had decided that I should see the worst shelters first. She gave the driver an address in the East End. I shall call it the Isle of Dog shelter, because people from the Isle of Dog, which is part of the East End, go there and because if the Germans do not know where so many people are concentrated under one not entirely adequate roof, I have no interest in telling them. I keep remembering that Dick Boyer reported that all the foreign news in *PM* is wirelessed daily to Berlin.

It was a long drive from the hotel. A long drive through the deserted, darkened streets of a city being bombed from the air is an experience. The driver never stopped to ask the way and proceeded at between twenty and thirty miles an hour. Strange objects rushed by us in the dark, buildings were suddenly silhouetted and the sky lit from time to time by the flashes of guns. Once a thin layer of clouds quite high up began to glow and everyone said, "Oh," and pointed. It was a flare coming down from a plane above. It went out when it hit the clouds.

London's traffic lights, red, green, and yellow like ours, were little red, green, or yellow crosses, visible only a few blocks away. They pulled us up at silent, deserted crossings, flicked us on again down empty boulevards. When we got to the Isle of Dog shelter we had some trouble finding the entrance. We walked along from the car, poking at dead shuttered windows and bolted doors with flashlights screened with our hands.

When we found it we went down a long damp flight of stairs at the bottom of which we found a small cubbyhole office with a counter window in it, several policemen and wardens standing about. Hilde took charge and told one that she was from the *Express*. He went away and came back with another man who was the head warden. We were all introduced formally. I asked him how many people there were in the shelter, which we could not see from where we stood.

He said, "Only about 8000 now. We should only have half that. That is, that's about the area that's approved. There were so many they just took over the rest of the cellar. One end hasn't much cover, you know. Just some sheds above it."

We started walking with him while Hilde and I asked him questions. Yes, as far as he could tell, the same people came back every night. No, they didn't have to queue up as much as they used to. Hilde explained that the queuing problem—people standing in line all day to go back into the shelter they had just left—had passed its acute stage. Something was being done about it. "Something" was a system of registration and numbering and assigning of places so an individual or a family needn't worry about getting their places back each night.

The warden said, "We call that end of the shelter the Ritz. We'll come back around by it."

We had been walking down a dimly lighted hall. Suddenly we came into a great cavernous room. It had been the subcellar basement of some commercial establishment and along one side were rows of wagons—flat-bottomed wagons with enormous wheels. In parts of the cellar there were counters raised a few feet from the ground.

It was impossible to take in the whole room. My memory of the place is confused and as I think of it the memory of individuals is stronger than the memory of the whole. You cannot take in the concept of thousands upon thousands of people sleeping in a dim-lit cave. The room into which we had just arrived was simply carpeted, blanketed, draped with people.

They lay in long rows the length of the counters. They filled the wagons with arms and legs and heads sticking over the tops. They sat propped against the wheels of the wagons. They balanced miraculously on the whiffletrees. They were under the wagons, packed into each other. I remember an old lady, bolt upright, in a kitchen chair with a black shawl wrapped around her.

In the open places they lay in rows with just room enough for us to walk down aisles lined by badly shod, twisted, sprawled feet. It was still only about ten o'clock, but about half of them were asleep. Most of those who were awake looked up with only mild curiosity. Many men had their hats on. A woman was sitting undoing her hair. Two women near her were whispering together. Here was a little island of reclining camp chairs. The people in them were old and fat and looked tired, even asleep.

We walked on and on, up one row and down another. It took the conversation and the questioning out of us. We just walked. Finally it came to an end, and beyond the roof raised up, disappeared into the black. A single lone blue light hung down. I smelled cigarette smoke. All of a sudden out of the noises came music, a guitar. Then singing. The warden said, "This is the social end. They can smoke here for another hour." The light was dimmer than it had been where people were sleeping.

I finally recognized a group of forty or fifty people

pressing in around the guitar player. The singers kept their voices down. They were singing American jazz songs with cockney accents. Beyond them I saw a kind of covered wagon in the rear end of which several men were busy. It was a canteen and it was just closing up. I went over and talked to one of the boys who was putting his equipment away. He said he had been working sixteen hours. He was too tired to be interested in telling me where.

I walked around the social hall. There were several hundred more people there, some of them talking, most leaning against the wall, smoking in silence. Another group began to sing in competition with the first. We moved off.

"It's not very pretty conversation," said Hilde, "but the problem of all these big shelters is the toilets. This place is the worst of all. How many have you got now?" she said to the warden. He stopped, looked at us, and frowned. "See for yourself," he said.

I looked where he pointed. I had not noticed what appeared to be a curtain of burlap ten or twenty feet long in front of the wall just beyond the sleepers' heads. I went over and looked. The standard toilet unit in an East End shelter is a three-foot square of floor screened to perhaps six feet high by burlap tacked to a little wooden frame. The front side is simply a curtain, pushed aside to enter. Inside there is a garbage can with chemicals in the bottom. Signs tacked on the front say "Men," "Women." They smell. In this shelter of 8000 people there were six of these burlap-screened conveniences for men, six for women. All that I saw were on the floor where the people slept.

We went back through other rooms as full of people. The whole experience shocked so that it numbed.

We came at last to the Ritz. The contrast between the Ritz and the rest of the shelter was very striking. In the

Ritz were long rows of new triple-tier bunks. The frames were solidly built and heavy burlap was nailed to them to sleep on. Each berth was permanently numbered. My head was about level with the top. The place was clean, better lighted, and not so many of the sheltered were asleep. It was a relief to be there. The people we talked to were obviously pleased with their lot. "Oh, yes, I have my number and I come back here every night."

"What about plumbing?" said Hilde to the warden. "They were going to put it in here. This is the place I'm yelling so much about," said Hilde to me. The warden grinned. "Yes, ma'am," he said, "they sent us a plumber and he's working over there." He pointed into a corner. "But," and he stopped smiling, "ma'am, he's such a little man."

Hilde said, "How many bunks have you got now?" He said, "About four hundred. They are very slow coming. Can't you do something about that, ma'am?" In the far end of the Ritz there was a first-aid bay.

"I want to show you a tube tonight, too," said Hilde. We stood talking to the warden for a while before we left.

I only remember that warden the way I remember other wardens I talked with. They have blended into a kind of composite memory of a young man, kindly, intelligent, cheerful, obviously able and competent, doing his best with an enormously complicated problem in human relations. He is the man on the firing line between the bureaucracy above and the people in his charge. There was no question about on whose side he was. He was on the side of the people he looked after.

A volunteer worker, he had no legal status. Policemen could order him about, his superiors could give him stupid regulations to enforce, turn a deaf ear to his requests or demands for equipment or tools with which to work. He stood there in the middle, never complacent.

He took what he had and did the best he could, talked and worked to do more. I told someone in England that London would one day erect a statue to the Unknown Air-Raid Warden. He agreed.

As we left the Isle of Dog shelter, Hilde said, "There you are. I know it's hard for you to believe it, but that place was much worse. There were many more people and no canteen and no place to smoke. And then there's the Ritz. And the warden's bunks are slow in coming and the man who is putting in the plumbing is such a little man. But that's the way we do things here. Slowly and often stupidly. But they'll get done. That man won't give up working to make that place better. You don't know what he's done already. But it's very terrible, that place, isn't it? And one day a bomb is going to hit it and there's going to be hell to pay."

We found our car and drove to the Liverpool Street Station tube. The Liverpool Street Station tube is the safest shelter in town. A tube—to translate—is a subway, and here the subway runs sixty feet underground.

An escalator runs down to it in a single long, straight descent. We came in out of the dark into the lighted station and found ourselves standing at the top of it. It was the second most extraordinary sight I saw in London. The entire length of this long stairway, which would reach six stories from the bottom of Macy's department store to the top—was packed—*two* people to a stair—with sleeping men. As in our own escalators, the banisters, when the stairs are in motion, move with the platform. Behind them are shelves, eighteen inches to two feet wide, slanting down parallel to the stairs at the same angle. Head to foot, to head to foot, to head to foot, the entire way down, both banister shelves were filled with more men asleep.

The men who slept on the stairs that had metal treads were contorted into unimaginable discomfort. Their rows of feet coming from opposite sides of the stairs left an irregular tread down the center, a few inches wide. Up and down this leather-walled path people were passing, coming up or going down.

The sight was so startling it produced no reaction except the sense that these people must be insane. Why did they choose to sleep sitting up along the stairs instead of going down into the tube? Neither Hilde nor Ben, who had seen these stairs before, seemed as impressed as I. I stood for a long time looking down the shaft. Finally we picked our way down.

The escalator opened on a subway platform. Along this platform, heads to the wall, feet toward the tracks, was another carpet of sleepers, absolutely solid, shoulder and thigh to shoulder and thigh. There was a train in the station, brightly lighted, with its doors open. In startling contrast to the packed horizontal humanity on the platform, only two or three people were sitting in the cars. There was a foot or two of clearance between the feet of the sleepers and the edge of the cars against the platform. I was about to say, "But why don't they go in the cars?" when its doors closed and it moved off away into the tunnel. The subway was operating as usual. The roar of the train's departure produced no visible effect on the sleepers.

We turned away from the platform and walked through some short connecting tunnels. By this time, after only a few hours of it, I found I had stopped being startled at the fact that every square foot of floor space except for the narrow aisles we moved along was packed with sleeping people. This was London by night. In the corridors of the British Broadcasting Building, the lobby of the Dorchester, or the Liverpool tubes—always, everywhere on the ground floor and below ground in big buildings, are people sleeping.

I don't know how to make you feel this picture. Think,

perhaps, of a New York apartment house in which you might live. Think how many people would be living there with you. Think where you would sleep if every night all of you came down in your elevators and made your bed in those mysterious basements normally guarded by the janitor. And think that this would not be just something you did one night when a ground-floor fire might have smoked you out, but that you did it every night until it became routine. Until you took it as a matter of course and thought nothing of it. Then think of a whole city doing this. Or try to think of it. It's doubtful if you can. I can't, even after having seen it. All I know is that within a day or two you accept it. That's the way it is. And you cease to be surprised by finding sleeping people wherever you go in London at night.

I said I ceased to be surprised at seeing sleeping people in odd corridors. The corridors we were walking through under the Liverpool Street Station led to the shelter I found the most extraordinary of all. Here a connecting link of the subway had been under construction when the war began. A short connecting link, not unlike the shuttle that connects Grand Central with Times Square in New York. Here in London the tunnels were finished but the tracks were never laid. Two circular tubes run side by side for a quarter of a mile—so that if you walk up one tube and turn the corner at the end you can walk down the other tube and have gone half a mile. The floors of these tubes were prepared for tracks. That is, they have concrete floors which flatten or truncate the circle at the bottom. From these floors the round sides of the tube rise to their widest point and then arch around to make the ceiling.

As I stood in the entrance of the tube I knew why men slept in the stair well. They slept there because there was no room for another human being in the tube down which I looked. Now, a human being in London comes perhaps five and half feet long and is not terribly thick through, even with an overcoat on. Fat ones take up more room, but skinny ones and children make up for them. The shape of the human being is also very adaptable. It can be twisted into an infinity of shapes.

So that when I say that not another human being could have been got in these tubes I am making a very strong statement. In their half-mile length were some blocks of toilet cans and about twenty feet which was beaver-boarded off to make a first-aid bay. But with the exception of spaces taken by toilets and the first-aid bay, my statement stands.

The night I was in the Liverpool Street tube you could not have got another human being into it without laying him directly on top of some other human being. This goes for the people lying back against the curving sides of the tube and for the people flat out along the floor.

Hilde Marchant, Ben Robertson, and I walked down one tube, around the corner and back the other. For exactly half a mile we walked, literally after each step having to find a place to put the next foot down without stepping on something human. As you might pick rocks to make stepping stones across a stream.

As you walk into the tube the sounds of its humanity come to meet you—the breathing and the snoring and the coughing. The three sounds blend, but are distinguishable. As you walk into the tube the air seems to meet you, push gently, then shove, and finally almost to wrestle with you. Toward the middle of each tube it is so heavy and dense you really feel as if you could take handfuls of it and pack them into mud pies.

Whether it was space or the time of night, most people in the tube seemed to be lying in positions that showed their faces. Perhaps it was the cumulative effect of walking past so many sleeping people—walking past them until they ceased to become merely a spectacle and began being human beings again. But walking past the people in the Liverpool Street tube made me cry. I thought, many people become children again when they are asleep. And all become individuals. They stop defending themselves from each other in their sleep, stop being frightened. They curled against each other, or they threw their arms out into each other's faces and the faces they struck turned away without knowing and they slept that way across one another.

The children kept stopping us. Most of the children have gone from London and there are not many in the shelters. But in the Liverpool Street tube there seemed to be a lot. Probably because it was so safe and people went a long way to make what was most precious to them safe. There were a lot of children in the Liverpool Street tube. They were very beautiful. Some put their arms around each other or around their mothers. There were several whole families of them, two, three, and four children, and seeing them lie by each other in ascending size you could tell how far apart they had been born.

It was late and the tube was sound asleep. We took a long time walking through it and it was a very moving experience. It did not add up to anything except that there were people and that they were very lovable.

We stopped in the first-aid bay. A wonderful stout woman who had been a practical nurse through three wars was in charge of it. It was to a modern hospital what the garbage-can toilets were to a modern sanitary toilet. There was a long table with white oilcloth that had been scrubbed through to the webbing. Along it lay a pitifully small store of tools and drugs. At one end was a cot. A small woman with gray hair sat cross-legged on it, rocking back and forth.

The nurse said, "She is in great pain, poor dear. She had a bad foot and a small boy ran into it and knocked

— 93 —

her down." The woman said nothing, but looked at us with large unhappy eyes and continued to rock back and forth. Hilde said, "Why don't you give her something?" "I haven't anything to give her." The big fat nurse who looked as if she would be jolly most of the time had an assistant and the assistant pointed to the things on the table and said, "She bought most of those with her own money."

When Hilde commented bitterly and angrily at this the nurse got a bag and took a letter out of it and showed it to us. It was from a doctor in answer to a request for aspirin. It was a nasty letter, written by a small and unpleasant man. It reminded the matron that she should remember that she was only a practical nurse and that first-aid posts were just what they were supposed to be, a place to give first aid until somebody who was competent could be called. The big fat nurse to whom it was written had a row of little colored ribbons sewn on her white uniform. They were decorations given her in service. The first-aid bay had no telephone in it. It served 4000 people who slept there every night.

Hilde was still furious. She said she was going to do something about it in the paper. She took down the name of the doctor who wrote the letter.

The first-aid post was halfway down the first tube. At the end of it, as we turned the corner into the second half, there was an emergency exit, guarded by two policemen. In the twenty or thirty feet nearest the exit the air was all right. We turned the corner and took a long time walking back through the second half of the tube. When we were in the first-aid bay we had looked at the case book. Three out of four entries were listed "mosquito bites." We noticed that a number of people showed signs of having been bitten. We thought, however, that the phrase "mosquito bite" was a euphemism.

We went on out through the connecting passageways

and up the long escalator, six stories high, along which the men sitting on both sides and stretched along the railings were still asleep. It was nearly 3 A.M. And we thought we'd call it a night.

We drove back to the Dorchester, not talking much. When we got to the Dorchester Ben Robertson said, "Would you like to see the shelters in the Dorchester?" We went in in our steel helmets, past the people who slept in the lobby. Ben didn't know where the shelters were, so a waiter who was just leaving took us down. We went past the empty kitchen and around a corner into what were once the Turkish baths. And there they were, the sleepers in the Dorchester shelter. A neat row of cots, spaced about two feet apart, each one covered with a lovely fluffy eiderdown. Its silks billowed and shone in the dim light in pale pinks and blues. Behind each cot hung the negligee, the dressing gown. By each cot the mules and the slippers. Alongside, the little table with the alligator-skin dressing case. The pillows on which the heads lay were large and full and white. The heads were heads. They did not sleep as well as the heads slept in the Liverpool Street tube. Even though it was 3 A.M. and we tiptoed, most of them raised up off the pillows and eyed us defensively. There was a little sign pinned to one of the Turkish-bath curtains. It said, "Reserved for Lord Halifax."

I have described the Isle of Dog shelter and the Liverpool Street Station tubes as we found them. They were and are scandalous. They are neither typical nor untypical. They are just there. Twelve thousand people a night sleep in the two of them.

But even after having seen the little improvement in the Ritz corner of the Isle of Dog shelter, I would have left London with a very wrong impression of life in the shelters had I stopped there. The next day we talked about what we had seen. People in the Home Security heard about it and Ellen Wilkinson, who is in charge under Herbert Morrison, called me up. One of her people got hold of Hilde Marchant and said it was unfair of her to show me only such places as I had seen the night before.

I respectfully declined the offer of an official guide, not because I suspected the Ministry of intentionally misleading me, but because I preferred to sacrifice knowledge of statistics for my own impressions. Hilde is not to be bullied. The Ministry is much more frightened of her than she is of it. She said, "In fairness, they are quite right. But you won't understand the problem we're up against until you have seen the worst shelters. After I've taken you to some more bad ones I will show you what they can do when they try, and why they ought to be ashamed of themselves for being so slow about it." So the next night after dinner we went out again.

Hilde said, "I think the place I'm taking you is the worst of all. I haven't been there for a month now, but it's under a brewery and it was simply unbelievable."

We reached the brewery shelter through a cobblestoned yard. It was in a district that had been heavily bombed and the guards were nervous. When we looked for the entrance with a flashlight they bellowed at us, "Put that bloody thing out. Where the bloody hell do you think you're at?" We put it out and felt our way in to the door.

A clean, sharp, yeasty smell met us. We went through the ground floor of the brewery and then down a stairway into the cellar beneath. We came into the big room in which several thousand people slept. We stood on some kind of raised platform, so that we looked out over them. I was instantly conscious of a sense of order—and of clear fresh air. The rows of sleepers were well separated and each had room to turn around. Dim, shaded, hanging lights lit the place as at twilight.

Hilde turned sharply on the warden. "But what's happened here?" she said. And then, "You're new here, aren't you?" The warden said he'd taken over three weeks ago. "It was a bloody mess then," he added. "I'll say it was," said Hilde. And to me, "But this is all changed," and to him, "What did you do?" He said he hadn't done anything except to limit the number of people he'd take and to make some rules. He said, "This is almost a wholly Jewish shelter and some of them wanted a place to pray, so I gave them a room over there in the corner. They like it."

"The toilets are still bad," he said, "but I've got them away to where they don't smell up the place and I got some air in here." Hilde said to me, "Well, there you are. That's very typical of the kind of thing that happens. This was really the foulest place of them all and this man's taken hold without anybody's help and made it decent, at least." I think it irritated her a little that her show was spoiled. But she was proud of the warden who had done such a good job. She said, "All right, then, now this is a lot better than it was, but now I'll show you what they can really do. And what they ought to do everywhere."

We drove into what appeared to be a business section and went into a lobby of an office building. We went down into a very deep cellar and I saw what she meant. The shelter was cut up into a number of rooms. The largest was well lit and along one side there was a permanent canteen which sold cigarettes and chocolate and served tea. There were several card games going on around bridge tables. All English pubs have, as standard equipment, a darts game: a cork target to hang on the wall and feather darts to throw at it. The shelter had its darts game and there was a good deal of gaiety going on in the group playing it. In another corner people were sitting reading.

"People can come in here and make themselves at home until they are ready to go to sleep," said the warden. The place had everything except numbered bunks. There were flush toilets; a very up-and-coming first-aid bay. People had plenty of room to sleep and they slept on mattresses.

The warden said, "They bring their blankets. We used to let them bring their own mattresses, but they're apt to have things in them, so we got mattresses to keep here for them." It was very clean. Most of the people I saw were obviously poor white-collar workers rather than laborers, but there were some men whose hands and bodies showed they did manual labor.

But the most typical shelter of all in England is not in a basement at all, but in a back yard. This is the one-family Anderson shelter that the government gives out to anyone with space to install it. And outside the city— and many places inside—the characteristic of the English house is its little garden. Four feet deep in this garden sets the Anderson shelter. I went into the East End again to see what one was like. We came back to the place where a land mine had gone off. We laughed because the little man we discovered beside his Anderson shelter was so very perfect we swore he had been planted there by the Ministry of Information. We should have had the dialogue on a sound track to use with the film *London Can Take It.*

He was a tough little cockney and he drove a switching engine along the Liverpool docks. His little house and garden were on the edge of the area the land mine had defaced—houses by the hundreds beginning half a block away were uninhabited. Directly across the street from him a bomb of 250 pounds—maybe 500 pounds—had blown a hole in the garden and wrecked the house behind it.

We asked him if he would show us his shelter because

I had come from America. He not only showed us his shelter but he took us all over the district and told us what had been hit where. He kept up a witty, running patter, a little over a third of which I was able to understand—it being cockney to begin with and full of local slang which kept Hilde laughing.

He said there were two things he didn't like about this war and the way he was treated in it. He said the anti-aircraft made him mad because they couldn't hit anything. He said he'd watched them and watched them. He wanted to see a German plane 'it and never 'ad, even though he worked out on the docks all day. And as to his own treatment, he told us he damn well wanted a tin hat. He said a bloke could do without a leg or an arm or this piece or that piece of 'im, but he couldn't do without 'is knob. He said he didn't see why the government couldn't give 'im and the other fellows that worked out on the docks steel helmets. Neither could Hilde or I. Hilde said she was going to make a campaign of *that*.

Like almost everyone he put in his Anderson shelter himself. An Anderson shelter is made of heavy galvanized cast iron, the kind you sometimes see on warehouse roofs. It is about four by eight feet square and five feet high, the top being arched to a circle. It is put in half submerged into the ground and then sandbags are piled around and over the top of it. Many people plant gardens on the roofs, flower gardens. It has other sandbags piled around its entrance. I climbed down into the little man's shelter. I could just get in. It had a concrete floor. He said concrete was hard to get but he had a friend who could mix it and all the people in the neighborhood got what cement they could and he and his friend went around and fixed up as many floors as they could. His shelter was quite dry. There were candles stuck on a little shelf and some odds and ends of cloth-

— 99 —

ing hung up. He said he had taken the bedding out to air it.

He told us he sent his wife and his son and daughter to the country, but his daughter, who was the older, had come back and was staying with some people down the street. And another married daughter was around the corner with her husband. He said, "Ain't no place for women, but they don't like to be away from 'ome and they come back." He said his was a good shelter and he slept very well there. But a lot of them were bad unless you had a good floor and knew how to fix it so the rain didn't come in.

Ben Robertson asked him if he was in the shelter when the bomb dropped across the street. He said, "Oh, yes. It shook quite a bit. But," he said, "I'm not afraid because I have it fixed so I can get out the back end if the front end caves in." I said, "What do you do when a bomb drops near you? Do you go out to see what happens?" he said, "Oh, yes. We have got a kind of a system. When there's a 'it everybody around comes out and we get together and go from one shelter to another to see if everybody else is all right, and to be sure the entrance 'asn't caved in and they can't get out.

"Then after we have checked up on everybody's being all right we go back into our 'oles." (Another time, talking about a friend, he used the sentence, "And every evening about five he goes 'ome to his ruins.")

Hilde said it was typical of London people, working out ways to look after each other like that. Ways that had nothing to do with government rules or regulations or even volunteer ARP wardens. Just people looking out for each other.

The little man said even his wife in the country would come back ever so often because she wanted to see that everything was in order in the house. He said he had no trouble looking out for himself.

He showed us almost with pride where the land mine had hit. It had touched no building, coming down in a yard near a factory. There had been several automobiles there and they were squashed in as if Gibraltar had fallen on them. Characteristically, the crater wasn't deep. But for blocks and blocks around there were little frame houses battered and windowless. It was very depressing to walk down the empty, uninhabited streets.

The little man who lived in the Anderson shelter halted suddenly and grunted with disgust, "There. See," he said pointing to the sky. "Why can't they 'it 'im?" We all stopped. It was a lone daylight raider. The plane could not be seen but its exhaust, crystallized in the cold upper air, wagged after it like a pollywog's tail as he twisted and turned. Half the antiaircraft guns in town seemed to be after him. Puffs of smoke were black above and below him.

"There! There! Now *why* can't they 'it 'im?" the little man kept saying over and over again, getting more and more excited. I found I felt exactly the same way. The German kept twisting and turning. He was going home toward the south and when last seen puffs were still pursuing him.

The little man shook his head. He sighed and said to me, "Well, I 'ope you 'ave a safe journey back to America."

We looked at a lot more shelters. They never ceased to interest me. They ran the whole gamut between the la-de-da one where they played bridge and darts and the cavern under the Isle of Dog. In almost every shelter we went Hilde noted improvements since she had been there last.

Only two generalizations were borne in on me. One was the extraordinary lack of preparation for the problem, considering the fact that although the *blitz* was only a couple of months old the war had been going on for over a year, and during all that year the English government had expected the bombing of civilians. The other was the fact that nowhere except in the Liverpool Street tubes and the deep office basement did I see what seemed to me really safe shelters. Nor did I see or hear of any concerted effort to dig or build deep shelters. There will inevitably be many shelters hit during the winter and it is a real miracle, considering the haphazard bombing, that more have not had direct hits from big bombs. There have been no real bomb massacres in shelters—yet.

In many things, but most of all in how the shelter problem has been met, there is in Britain this curious paradox: no one did anything but talk until the problem became acute, but when it did become acute, at precisely the point at which the acuteness would have panicked most people, the British have surprisingly settled down to solving it. They do not appear to have any capacity at all for foresight, for seeing the course of events a long way off and preparing for it. They must wait until the terrible things have actually happened before doing anything about it. Thus, despite a year of war there was really no shelter provision at all until the bombs actually came down, and then they were makeshift. And no one did anything about their overcrowding until it was fantastic.

Now in England everyone knows that in January and February it will be very cold and damp and English shelters are not heated and many, many thousands of people sleep on the damp cellar floors with only a blanket under them, and yet while everyone in London talks about it, there's no evidence of anyone doing anything about it. Nor would I expect them to do anything about it until after there have been some dreadful epidemics. Nor will there be deep shelters unless and until the Germans drop many more of their very large bombs and there have been bad casualties.

I came back in the plane with an American who had just come from Hamburg, and he told me that day and night the Germans were digging deep shelters for the residents—against the day when Britain has more planes with which to bomb. That is the German way, no matter under what kind of government. It's not the English way. When the English do get around to doing something about their problems they may as often as not do something spectacularly good, as witness the organization of their bomb fire-fighting department which I am about to describe. Or the RAF that is probably the finest fighting unit that the world has ever known. But the RAF was a neglected branch of the service till the bombers were actually over England. I don't know enough about these things to make any real sense, but I give you the paradox to explain. It's strikingly apparent in many phases in England.

VIII

FIRES, FEAR, AND FREUD

THE FIRE DEPARTMENT

ONE NIGHT we drove across the river to see the Fire Department. Its headquarters are in an enormous modern blocklike building, almost as good a target as the Battersea Power Station, commonly known as Lotts Road Station. Germans keep trying but they have not hit it yet. Ben Robertson told me the city was divided into two districts—east and west of the river—and that the head of each was a young man in his middle thirties. Their names are Fordham and Blackstone. He called one of them up and we were invited over.

We found Messrs. Fordham and Blackstone in a comfortably furnished apartment on the seventh floor. New York has never seen fire chiefs like them. They are university career men in fire fighting. At one end of the drawing room in which we sat, while one of them went off to find some beer for us, hung a large oil painting of Mr. Fordham in uniform—he was in mufti when he received us—holding his enormous brass helmet in the crook of one arm. It was done by a very good painter. They talked intelligently, simply—with wit and charm. They told us that there had been about 20,000 fires in

London since the *blitz* began—or rather 20,000 big enough to be worth counting. A Fire Department of a few thousand had grown to 20,000 men on active duty with 10,000 men in reserve and in training. (In New York City, 10,413 firemen.) They explained that it took a little time to train men, but that even more important was experience in the field. They were very modest about their work. Ben reminisced with them about the fires on the famous night of September 15. Ben said he had never understood how they put them out. Mr. Fordham thought for a minute and answered: "You know, I was pretty surprised myself when they did go out. You know, there were so many mains out. It was rather hard to get water."

I knew one reason it was bad, because when bombers light a fire they always come back and use it for a target to bomb some more.

There have been over 2000 firemen killed or wounded on duty in London since it began. Two thousand are a lot of firemen.

Mr. Fordham explained to us about the system that already has been described by correspondents, the dispersal of apparatus outside of fire stations, on street corners. Going about London you see them everywhere. The standard gear is a small two-walled hose truck. Attached to the rear of a car is a trailer. The car is sometimes a truck built for the purpose, with a covered tonneau in which there are seats for the firemen—lengthwise as in a patrol wagon—and a place for tools and chemicals. As often as not the car that pulls the hose trailer is a commandeered taxicab with the gear piled into the rear seat where the passengers ordinarily ride. Dispersal of personnel and equipment is the great lesson of this war—for everything from civilian shelters, hospitals, factories, planes, and airports to fire apparatus to put out bomb fires.

Mr. Fordham asked if we would like to see the **control room**. I said we would. He said: "We have a good view from the roof. Would you like to walk around up there first?"

We went up to look around. There were a number of German planes in the air and you could hear them more clearly than in the street. The spotters on the roof corners were alternately watching them and looking out over the surrounding rooftops. Everywhere over London these watchers are on duty every night, all night. The barrage was heavy and all around us were flashing **guns** and above us the flashes of bursting shells. Two or three German planes together droned across to us. The searchlights tried to find them. Mr. Blackstone said: "They keep trying to hit us here."

After a while we went in and took the elevator down to the control room.

It was a very deep cellar. I don't think any kind of bomb could have got to it. As we walked into the room on the left we saw the wide sweep of a multiple-place telephone switchboard, manned by firemen. They were sitting on stools, twisting idly from side to side. There were no cords in the switchboard. Nothing was happening. Directly in front of us across the middle of the room sitting in little cubicles with their backs toward us were half a dozen girls, telephone equipment on their heads. They were all knitting. Mr. Fordham said: "When a call comes in, the switchboard transfers it to one of the girls who takes down the details. There are no bells. The switchboard attracts their attention by flashing a light."

A light flashed above one girl's head. I looked rapidly at the switchboard. One of the firemen was obligingly flashing the light to demonstrate for us.

I thought of all those planes I had heard passing overhead. I felt nervous. If there was a bomb fire I wanted to go to it, but I knew I would be frightened. We walked on past the girls into the far half of the room. And on two large walls were enormous maps of London. The most interesting-looking was covered with hundreds and hundreds of thumb tacks with heads in different shapes and colors. Four or five alert and intelligent young men stood about or sat at tables in the center of the room. We were all introduced. Mr. Fordham said to one: "This is your show. I wonder if you wouldn't like to explain it?"

The man did.

He said: "You see, this map shows the disposition of every piece of equipment in London and as the fires come in the equipment moves. All the other equipment in London can be moved so that the city is always covered and the disposition of pieces is always the most efficient possible. Now, if it's just what we call a ten-pump fire we will just move up a few pieces to take the place of the ones that have gone to the fire. These"—and he pointed—"are district lines. If one district is having a really bad time it can draw on the districts around it. This whole map you see is only for what we call the City of London Fire District. Suburban districts are kept track of just like this. The boards are all on the other side. If we were in real trouble here we might call on them for apparatus. Or vice versa. The whole system is very flexible. We can move very rapidly."

I probably use inaccurate terms but this was the gist of it. I marveled. I have never seen such obviously smooth efficiency in an undertaking on such a scale and so new. For the *blitz* began in August and it still was October. All this that was now such a solid, simple, effective system was only yesterday emergency. Terrible emegency. I thought to myself, "The English are the most extraordinary people in the world. They are so unbelievably slow and unforesighted about some things, and yet they work out this marvel overnight. One month their Fire

Department is an old-established bureaucracy. It must have been always well run, but it had only a few thousand men. And its equipment like our equipment at home was heavy and ponderous and relied on perfect water distribution. And then the next month there must have been more fires in a week than there had been in a year before, and tens of thousands of new men—a whole organization to be revamped—equipment installed, men trained, routine worked out. And here it all is—as smoothly run as the dispatcher's office in the Grand Central Terminal in New York."

I didn't count them, but there couldn't have been over twenty or twenty-five people in the control room. It didn't cover much more area than the big newsstands in the 42nd Street side of the Grand Central. Yet these few men in this little room directed an army that licked the *Luftwaffe*. They could put fires out faster than all the aerial armadas backed by all the lethal chemists could start them. I told them that I couldn't believe my own eyes. It was such a beautiful system. They were so modest about it they seemed shy. One of them said: "It works rather well."

We looked at the other boards. They showed us the records. He talked some more about the night of September 15. It must have been hell.

Mr. Fordham said: "This board also records the fires that are burning in London now."

It was empty, except for two small green dots in one corner. I thought again of the bombers flying back and forth five miles overhead. I asked if these were big fires. He said: "Oh, no, no. Just two little ones on the edge of town."

We stood around talking quite a while, but no more calls came in. The firemen at the switchboard continued to wriggle in their chairs. The girls continued to knit. It was about one o'clock in the morning. We went back up to the ground floor and ran into a fire pole on which the firemen who slept above slide to the engines parked where we were. My friend, the Wing Commander in the RAF, was with us. He asked if he might slide down the fire pole. He said he had never slid down a fire pole and always wanted to. We all went upstairs. Mr. Fordham explained how to hold the pole. Not with your hands, but in the crook of one arm. Down we slid one by one. After a while we thanked Mr. Fordham for the time he had given us. We went out and got in our car and drove away.

Just before dawn I was awake and looked out over London from the Dorchester. The "all clear" had sounded. The city was silent, black.

Just for fun I clipped the German official communiqué describing the bombing of London on the night we spent in the Fire Department's headquarters. Here is what it said: "Squadrons of German bombers again dropped many bombs yesterday on London, obtaining hits particularly near the West End district and Waterloo Station. Great tongues of flame and new fires were observed."

The accuracy of this communiqué parallels the accuracy of every other German communiqué I checked personally while I was in England.

THE CENSORSHIP

"The General" printed a story in *PM* recently about censorship. The moral was don't believe what you hear from Europe unless it is confirmed by a neutral correspondent who has no ax to grind. It's a good piece and I have made a note that we should reprint it from time to time as a reminder. But it is based on observation and analysis of the aggressive Fascist and Nazi propaganda machine, and if taken literally as applicable to *all* foreign news, I think it's misleading.

I found in Great Britain, for instance, no evidence to believe that we in America had been either intentionally misled or confused or that, considering all things, any unreasonable amount of news had been withheld. The news that we don't get is contemporary news of military operations or military or civilian damage in England. I use the word "contemporary" because it appears the British policy to confirm any bad news several days later.

Because it's important in understanding news from abroad to understand the filtering process through which it passes, this is a piece about the British censorship.

The censorship is (1) a policy and (2) a large body of partially trained men to administer it. There is no such thing as "the Censor." The head censor in London is an extremely charming and intelligent ex-lawyer named Monckton, who says, "I certainly never thought I'd find myself in this job." Hundreds of men work for him, opening letters, reading cables before they're sent, blue-penciling copy in newspaper offices. His is part of the larger organization of the Ministry of Information, other channels of which do such creative propaganda as inspiring the film, *London Can Take It*, writing short-wave broadcasts to be translated into Arabic, etc. The treatment of newspaper copy cabled from London varies enormously with individual censors over whose desks it passes, and correspondents, for example, will change from one cable company to another in order to do business with a more understanding censor, each telegraph company having its own man assigned to it from above.

Chief Censor Monckton told me—and there's an abundance of evidence that it's true—that the present policy of the British Government is that the more truth it can let out the better, and that in this phase of the war conservative, accurate claims are simply the best policy. When he used the phrase "can let out," what he meant was "can let out without aiding the enemy."

It's not immediately apparent to the layman how news can aid the enemy until he has been on the field. I admit to having been suspicious of the vagueness in which cables about damage to London were worded—suspicious that detail was omitted to conceal more extensive damage than was acknowledged. Having been in London I now admit that I would not alter or circumvent the censorship in this respect even if I could. Because to print in the paper next morning where a big bomb fell last night is, of course, simply to spot or mark the accuracy of the bombing, for the Germans. And that I have no interest in doing. I admit also to having entirely new ideas about posters all over Britain admonishing civilians to keep their mouths shut—because information given to men who are trying to kill you is suicidal in the most literal sense.

I have, in these pieces I am writing, avoided giving specific references, whenever I could imagine specific references might aid and abet the enemy war effect. I have not, for instance, given the correct address of the big shelters I visited, for the obvious reason that there are maps of London in Berlin.

After I had been in London a few days I asked a dozen American correspondents to lunch and we discussed the censorship with no English present. Not one of the journalists there but had his or her inventory of gripes or complaints about this or that stupidity. A damn fool in Dover refused to let Robertson report a battle he saw in which two British planes were shot down, and seven Germans. Another in London bottled the news that the King's former residence had been hit and that the King had said, "Well, now I'm a real Londoner." Things like that.

As one of the things I wanted to find out was how

much news they—who knew infinitely more than I—had been unable to transmit to America, I did my best to egg them on. But instead of getting any startling revelations I got, believe it or not, a defense of the English censorship from the Americans who fought with it every day. It was the Americans who explained to me that to tell what bombs were falling at what addresses at what time might very conceivably improve the accuracy of the bombing of London—the last thing that anyone in that room wanted to be party to.

The fact that there's a censorship at all, and that it's composed of so many individuals bright and dull, helpful and irritable, wise and foolish—and that any censor in doubt will prefer to censor too much rather than too little—has the cumulative effect of dampening and flattening out copy—and undoubtedly conceals more than it means to. I did not write when I was in England, not because I wanted to put one over on the censor by waiting until I came back, but at least partially because I knew that I would have to argue about and justify a lot that I wrote and it all seemed like too much work. The correspondents who write to the American newspaper readers every day do have to argue and justify, often lose the best phrases in their copy because a stupid man does not understand them. But the moral of all this is that the censorship that is at work today is really more of a chronic nuisance than a menace to truth and accuracy in news.

Relations between the censorship and a resident writer in London are quite intimate. Everyone knows everyone. The right of appeal to a higher bureau is respected, as is the right to argue. An ex-newspaper managing editor named Brebner handles relations with American correspondents. He gets things done for them and they like him.

I think the American people are much more frightened

both of the British censorship and of British propaganda than they need be. Neither is really mysterious. It is definitely not a propaganda based, as the Fascist operation is based, on disrespect for the truth. The policy is not based, as the Fascist policy is based, on the dynamic lie, the Hitlerian lie, the lie that the Germans aim to make the truth by saying it so often and emphatically.

Have I said anywhere that I now have entire confidence in the accuracy and conservativeness of the RAF's claims as to how many German planes they have shot down and how many of their own they have lost each day? I came to take it so much for granted—after checking several days' communiqués at the airports themselves —that I almost forgot to mention it.

How the communiqués are compiled, what constitutes a "confirmed claim," I will write about when I get to the RAF itself.

ANNA FREUD AND DR. GLOVER

One afternoon I went out to see Anna Freud, the daughter of the late great Sigmund Freud, the scientist who created psychoanalysis and whom the Germans drove from Austria to die in England. I had letters to her from New York. I wanted to see her because she is a psychoanalyst herself and because from her and other psychiatrists I wanted what scientific evidence they had of the effect of the bombing on the emotional balance of the population. I had also heard that she was organizing a clinic for the study of bomb shock, a clinic to study particularly its effect on mothers and young children.

I found her house, the house in which her father died, a twenty minutes' drive from the center of the city. It is an undistinguished two-story suburban house set a few feet back from the road.

Anna Freud is a small, dark, handsome woman with an alert and thoughtful face. She received me in an attic studio which looked out onto a charming garden at the rear of the house. I told her why I wanted to talk to her. She said that she had not got her clinic started yet but that everything was arranged. The city of Westminster was giving her a building. Her assistants were to be men and women she had worked with in Austria and they were going to give her only women and children who had already shown some signs of fear and strain. She hoped the center would be helpful to them.

She said, "You have never seen anything like these people. You wouldn't believe it unless you lived here. They are so calm, and they take it all so well."

She said that the psychiatrists of London had met the week before to talk about the very subject I was asking her about. She said the retreat from Dover had produced many cases of shell shock amongst the soldiers and sailors who took part in it. But that none of the psychiatrists who discussed it together had a single true case of shell shock to report amongst the civilians of London. There were no nervous breakdowns that could be directly attributed to the bombing. "In a great city," she said, "there are always people whose lives become too difficult for them to handle, but we cannot see that they have been aggravated by the bombing."

I asked her about her own work. She said her day was full with private patients. The private patients of an analyst are not usually people without emotional difficulties. I asked her about her own patients. She said there was one girl whom she was treating whose life was in a very bad mess. She said the girl now worked driving an ambulance. She'd had a very bad bombing recently. The day after it she was in a very agitated mental state, excited and overtalkative. And the day after that, too—only not so sharply. But the third day she was quite normal again. The experience of the bombing had left no mark. Anna Freud said she thought it was a good case by which to judge the effect of bombing on someone already neurotic.

She went back to talking about the English with whom she had come to live. She said, "The bombing is really quite bad around here." I was surprised, because I had not noticed damage driving out. She took me to the window looking over the garden and pointed. I saw for the first time that a big building standing opposite and beyond was no more than a shell. Its roof was gone, its insides blown out. On either side the houses were windowless. She said there had been a lot of other hits around her. "I must show you my collection of shrapnel and bomb fragments picked off the roof or raked off the lawn." I saw it later. She kept it in a bowl in the front hall. Eighteen inches in diameter, it was piled nearly a foot high with sharp, irregular fragments of shell and bomb casings.

She said, "I know everyone around here very well. No one seems really bothered by this. They do not grumble or complain." I asked her what happened when people were bombed out of their houses. She said, "Hereabouts they are always taken in, if not by relatives or friends by someone else. They make the best of it."

She said her maids did not sleep in the house and that she made it a rule that they leave early enough to be home before the blackout. "But," she said, "they often do not go. They want to finish doing this or that or finish tidying up. They are utterly unafraid. And," she said again, "it gets really quite bad, you know."

I asked her where she slept. She said she slept in the house but that she went down on the ground floor with the three others who lived there and they slept on mattresses. She said, "I don't sleep up here because the windows might blow in and the shrapnel sometimes breaks the roof."

I said this was the first suburban house I had been in in London and would she show me what she did about air raids. She said, "Oh, I would like to show you. You must see the way the people here live in it. First, outside the door you must have noticed the pail of sand and the little galvanized-iron scoop at the end of the wooden handle. The sand is to put out incendiary bombs. The scoop to put on the sand or pick up the bomb before it gets really hot. You buy them at the store. There are many different kinds. Everyone has them. Then down by the door you will notice four suitcases standing in the hall. You can tell how many people live in each house when you come in by the suitcases standing in the hall. You pack them with some clothes and anything you want really to take with you in case the house is blown down or a time bomb falls in it. Then on each stair landing you will find another pail of sand and perhaps a pail of water with a bicycle pump beside it—to pump the water on the fire, you know." And here we stepped out into the hall. "You see the ladder—always left up to reach the roof so that when you hear incendiary bombs fall you can go up and put them out."

It was all exactly as simple and as matter of fact as that. And in every house into which I subsequently went I found similar routines as simply taken. She told me the only thing she missed in the war was her radio. "Without it it is hard to get news." I asked her where it was. She said, "They took it away because I am an alien. But," and she laughed, "you see how badly I'm treated. I live in this pleasant house and I go wherever I like and buy whatever I like in the stores. And there are thousands like me who now have no country but this."

We talked some more about the clinic. She said it was going to need money when it was going. I said I would like to help her get it in the U. S. She said she would be very grateful. Her address is 20 Mares Field Gardens, London, N.W. 3.

It was getting dark and she thought I should go. I said I would like to talk to her again. She said she would like to hear how I found things after I had been in London a little longer. I tried to reach her again. Something happened to the telephones that day. I think of her calm and neat little house and of the big bomb that missed it by a garden's length and of the pile of shrapnel she has raked from the lawn and of what she felt about the courage of the people in London. I think she is quite right about the matter-of-fact courage with which they're standing what they feel they have to stand. Nothing I saw or no one I talked to refuted it. I thought also that she is not without courage herself, that it would not be difficult for her to move away from London into the country. I thought that while hers was only one house— even though a house to which the great Freud came to live and die—there must be scores of thousands of simple, undistinguished little houses like it in which the sand buckets stand outside the doors and the packed suitcases inside, around which man-made steel and chemical destruction falls and whose people, amazingly, go the even tenor of their ways, the calmness of their souls undisturbed. I thought that I doubted if Adolf Hitler understood these things.

The other psychiatrist whom I went to see in London was Dr. Edward Glover, his offices on Wimpole Street. I had a letter to him from Dr. Gregory Zilboorg in New York. I spoke of my serious interest in the effect of the bombardment on the morale and emotions of civilians and Dr. Glover did me the courtesy of talking as to a professional. To what Anna Freud had told me he added these things:

That when the bombing began he and some other

psychiatrists had organized a clinic to be opened three days a week to receive from shelters and hospitals those individuals who were being broken down emotionally by the terror. He said that they thought they would begin with three days a week to see what happened. They thought it might be quite bad.

"And was it?" I asked.

Dr. Glover shrugged his shoulders. "It's hard to believe," he said. "We closed it down because we had no patients."

I asked him how he accounted for it. He said, "It is a very interesting thing. One can only speculate. But I believe it is because the experience of being bombed is so universal."

I said I didn't quite understand.

He said, "Well, I will put it this way. In the last war when men were in the trenches in France and they had only a little rest behind the lines between bombardments, there was always far away behind them the peaceful countryside in France or England—if anything happened to them they knew that that was where they would go. So when it got too much for them things happened. A trigger finger became paralyzed. A man lost his sight. But now these people in London, for instance, each day read that Scotland and the Midlands have been bombed. There are no green fields for them to go to in their imagination. Since there is no escape they accept reality and when they accept it they get used to it.

"But," he added, "I'm not really sure that's right. It is simply extraordinary but it is quite real. People are not made depressed or ill by being bombed."

He thought for a minute. He said, "Of course, there is also the difference between the night and the day. As long as there is always daylight when things are not so bad it makes a great difference. People throw themselves into the work there is to be done. I have watched it in

— 118 —

myself. When it began it was a tremendous experience and I would work about the city helping get people out of bombed buildings; studying what was happening until I got so tired I got careless. I had some narrow escapes. I found when I got through I didn't care where I slept or that I was sleeping in dangerous places. I had to say to myself, 'Look here, you are too old for this sort of thing. Hold yourself back.' "

Dr. Glover is an enormous man and very Scotch. He speaks with a broad burr. He is perhaps fifty-five years old. He said that when it began they wanted him to go into the Ministry of Information and he turned the job down. He said, "I work with them but if I took an official position I couldn't call my soul my own. I can now. For instance, when it started people lost their heads a little and began locking everybody up. They took two or three of my assistants who were foreigners. I could go and raise hell with them and I did. My people are where they belong—back with me now. When a big thing like this happens lots of people lose their heads and do stupid things."

I told Dr. Glover that I'd seen the Ministry of Information's secret report on morale—a report gathered weekly from thirty-some individual fact-gathering agencies, some operating like our own Gallup and *Fortune* polls, some the reports of trained observers, police, intelligence officers. I said I was amazed at the frankness of these reports, which I saw mimeographed and which therefore must go to many people. They recorded criticisms of government policies, mistrusts of holdovers from Chamberlain's Cabinet such as Lord Halifax, anti-Semitism which seemed to be waning after an ominous rise, fear in Ireland not of the Germans but of the English, the worry of some air-raid wardens that the country's morale would not stand the cold of the winter in damp shelters.

I told him I was amused at some of the rumors and

superstitions that were recorded, such as that to display a captured Messerschmidt to raise money for the Spitfire Fund was to invite enemy bombing. And the arguments over whether the balloon barrage worked and what about the antiaircraft accuracy. Of the intelligence of the criticisms—of the Ministry of Information itself among other institutions.

He said he thought the reports did a good job and that they showed no weakening in morale but rather a strengthening. He said that the reports from Ireland showed that there was growing a "grudging admiration" for the way the English took it.

I said I thought the government had certainly not been forethoughtful about providing shelters. He threw his hands up into the air. "Things have to happen before anything is done about them in this country. But then something is done. The shelters are getting better. All the doctors are frightened about the winter, of course. You know the winters are not bad here through December, but January, February, and March are verra, verra mean. There is a lot of work to be done before then." I don't think I met a man in England who seemed to look forward to that work with as much gusto as this huge, burly psychiatrist.

He said, "There's a lot more thinking to be done about why these people take it as well as they do—scientific thinking, I mean. We must wait to see more of the cumulative effect. But as long as the Germans keep bombing the whole island and as long as the RAF keeps them away from here by day, I don't worry about them."

IX

WINSTON CHURCHILL, ERNEST BEVIN, AND CLAUDE COCKBURN

THE PRIME MINISTER

Two DAYS before I left, my appointment with Mr. Churchill came through. He would see me at 11:30 A.M.

I was excited about the prospect of meeting the man on whom so much history depends. Since I had been in London I had come to feel quite definitely about what the English call The War Effort—that it was less of a one-man show than I had believed. Before I flew to London I had felt that the weight of England was too precariously balanced on the health and success of a single man. Now I found it impossible to think of the English ceasing their effort to defeat Hitler regardless of what happened to their Prime Minister and not withstanding his obviously dictatorial position in the government. But that did not make me any less curious about what he was like.

Ten Downing Street is a short alley opening off Whitehall, which is a busy avenue along which busses run and in the center of which there are lanes of parked taxis. There is no exact parallel in New York geography, although you might think of it as being on a side street

just off Park Avenue in the Forties. The government of
the British Empire is a compact little operation in the
center of its largest city. Now that this city is being
bombed in the air, the Empire's government is being
bombed, a central target well known to aviators in
Berlin. Expanded war operations have taken over such
modern skyscrapers (of eight and ten and fifteen stories)
as the International Nickel Building, the tower that
housed the College of London, etc. But 10 Downing
Street remains 10 Downing Street in the middle of it all.

The entrance is barricaded with barbed wire and sandbags, and sentries are on guard. I walked down the alley
and rang the bell at the side of the famous door. Its brass
was neatly polished. A butler opened it. We crossed the
hall and my friend Brendan Bracken, who used to publish financial journals in the city and is now one of the
Prime Minister's top secretaries, was standing before a
small desk. He is a medium-sized man with a large head
set in a still-larger halo of bright red hair, which appears
to stand on end and wave. He looks a little like a red
version of *The New Yorker*'s Harold Ross.

He said, "I think the Prime Minister is waiting," and
we went out of the room and down a steep stairway and
to a girder-roofed cellar basement.

It had a Dutch-tiled fireplace on one side and was
fitted as a temporary secretarial office with typewriters
on tables. A young lady was sitting at one, doing nothing. Mr. Bracken went into the room beyond, came back,
and said: "I thought he was going to see you down here
but he wants you up in the Cabinet room." We went
back upstairs.

The room in which the British Cabinet meets is a
handsome room with big windows on two sides and a fireplace on the third. The big windows were covered with
wire and a small pane in one was broken. There are
bookcases between the windows. Each new member of

the Cabinet gives a book. Most of the room was taken up with a long mahogany table at which places were set for Cabinet ministers. Each had his own desk equipment of an inkwell, blotter, pencils and pens and paper. In the center of the table the long way, with its back to the fireplace, was a chair that was larger than the rest which was obviously the Prime Minister's. On the wall space that was not filled with bookcases were hung portraits. At the far end of the room on a table rested an enormous picture projector which someone told me later was called an epidiascope. It pointed toward the screen which had been hung over the bookshelves opposite. Bracken said it was there so that aerial photographs of bomb damage in Germany could be enlarged and thrown up on a screen for the Cabinet to see.

The Prime Minister came striding in. Brendan Bracken said, "I want to introduce Ralph Ingersoll. He's been a good friend of England's." We shook hands and Brendan left.

My first impression was that Winston Churchill was smaller, rounder, neater, and redder than I imagined from his pictures. His eyebrows, his rusty hair, are thin red. I am quite tall myself so that people sometimes look small to me who do not look small to other people. The Prime Minister looked very small to me. I found his voice and conversation milder than I had anticipated. He sat down with his back to the fire and I sat alongside of him.

One of the things I wanted most to bring from England was a first-hand message from the Prime Minister to the American people. And after all I am a journalist and there would be news in such a statement. I wasn't to have my cake. As soon as I began asking him questions, the Prime Minister said that this message must be a "private conversation." I tried to argue with him. Prime Ministers don't argue with well.

He turned me down gracefully but definitely, remarking reasonably that expressing oneself accurately was difficult and that when he had something to say publicly he liked to think a great deal about it and work it out in his own way. So we talked as one must talk with the President of the U. S., "not for publication." We talked for half an hour.

I can't honestly say that I came away very much wiser although all my questions, most of which asked his opinion on various phases of international politics and the probable costs of the war and what he felt about America's relations to it, he appeared to be answering simply and frankly.

I can only say this about his answers: nothing he said contradicts the statements I have set down in a piece I have written about the politics of the British Government in its war efforts. I would like of course to give you as much of my conversation with Mr. Churchill as I ethically could. I don't think he would mind my passing on the strong feeling I had that I was talking to a sincere man and one who is entirely sure of his values—who knows exactly what life means to him, of what he approves or disapproves. I did not find him either a subtle or an intellectual man. Someone in London said he was at heart a cavalry officer with great courage. I wouldn't be surprised. He isn't a college professor.

When answering questions he has an odd trick of going on answering question one a long time after question two has been asked, then suddenly moving the conversation on, perhaps interrupting himself in the middle of a sentence, and then when I was thinking he would be through with question two and ask question three, he would go right on with the answer to two. I enjoyed my conversation with him, although I found I was anxious all the time I was talking to him. I kept wondering whether I was getting the most out of it because there were so many things I wanted to know from him. He looked well and nervously energetic. Several times during the conversation he got up, stood with his back to the fire, walked a step or two, came back and sat down— talking all the time. Finally he looked up at the clock on the mantel and said, "I am afraid I have to go now." We walked out together to his secretary's office.

In the middle of our conversation an alert had been sounded. The sirens had gone off at the pertinent moment when I asked him: "What are you going to do with this war after you have won it?" When we got into the secretary's office Mr. Churchill said, very firmly, "You are to stay here until we find out where those planes are. If they are near by, this young man will take you down to the shelters." I said, "Please don't bother. I don't mind at all." Mr. Churchill said, "No. No. You are not to go out until we've found out where that plane is. While you are here you are in my charge and you will do as I say."

He told the secretary to call up and get a report. He said to me, "They know very well where this house is and they keep trying to hit it. They put one not very far away once." The secretary and I stood awkwardly. He said, "Good-by," went to the door, turned, and said, "I would like you to know that I appreciate the things you have written." And then he left abruptly.

The planes turned out not to be near by. I waited some minutes, chatting with his secretary. He was a dark slim young man in his middle thirties who said he had been secretary to Mr. Chamberlain before he was secretary to Mr. Churchill. I said Mr. Chamberlain wasn't popular in this country, and he said, "Ah, that's a pity. I think he was very much misunderstood." When he said "was" I remembered that I had learned the day before that Mr. Chamberlain was dying.

He said, "I have never known a mind as brilliant as

Mr. Chamberlain's. It was unbelievably quick and clear, incisive."

I turned the conversation back to Mr. Churchill. I asked the secretary if he would tell me Mr. Churchill's routine because I said I was interested in how a man ran a war. The secretary said, "He has an enormous amount of energy, you know. I think the thing about Mr. Churchill that has not been emphasized enough is his military knowledge and experience. It is very rare, you know, that a Prime Minister can talk to his generals on a basis of equality. Mr. Churchill has them in here and he knows what they are talking about."

I asked if they ever talked back and argued with him. He said: "Oh, my heavens, yes."

I talked to a lot of people about Mr. Churchill and I already knew much of his routine. He no longer sleeps in 10 Downing Street, although I understand he left protesting. The Cabinet thought it too dangerous. What he does do—or did while I was in London—is get up as early as seven o'clock in the morning, dress hurriedly, go to 10 Downing Street, go down to the basement cellar where his bedroom is arranged, get undressed, and get back into bed. And he has his breakfast, which is enormous and apt to be built around the whole bird. There he reads the morning papers and selected mail and dispatches. And there he dictates to "two tame female secretaries" for several hours. So that when he met me at 11:30 he had just dressed again.

There is a Cabinet meeting before luncheon every day. The generals, admirals, and air marshals are apt to come in then.

Late in the afternoon he goes down into his cellar bedroom and sleeps again before dinner. When he told me that he slept in the afternoon he giggled apologetically. After dinner he works on until twelve or one, sometimes until two or three in the morning. He has no thought for anything except winning the war.

Everywhere I went in London people admired his energy, his courage, his singleness of purpose. People said they "didn't know what Britain would do without him." He was obviously respected. But no one felt he would be Prime Minister after the war. He was simply the right man in the right job at the right time. The time being the time of a desperate war with Britain's enemies. Everyone remarked that he loved his job and that he had risen to his terrific responsibilities brilliantly. Two personal failings were criticized—first that while he could be and was utterly ruthless in letting nothing come ahead of the war effort, he had a weakness toward people who were old friends and associates. He found it very difficult to bring himself to remove them even when he knew they were failing him. The second weakness was the one the secretary touched on, his penchant for playing general himself. It was felt that he might be too much of a cavalry officer and have too little of the technical knowledge so important in a technical war.

I have no opinion on either score myself but simply pass these remarks on as the comments of intelligent men who know Mr. Churchill well and who admire and respect him despite these things.

Even his critics had to admit that his recent promotions in the air and the Navy belie the first, and that whoever was responsible for it at least some of the credit for the amazing technical accomplishments of the RAF must be passed on to the boss. I think I should also say that with all the talk there is in the world of Mr. Churchill as a dictator I found a minimum of evidence in London to confirm it. Dictatorial powers he has. But much more typical than signs of their being imposed are demands from below that they be used for this, that, or the other purpose.

After I talked with the Prime Minister's secretary a few minutes more we shook hands and I went out. I looked up. There were no signs of any raiders in the sky. I wondered whether Mr. Churchill had gone out onto the streets himself after insisting that I stay close to the shelter. I suspect it would have been just like him.

ERNEST BEVIN

Ernest Bevin is the Minister of Labor in Mr. Churchill's Cabinet. Before the war his job was the Transport Workers Union and he was commonly acknowledged to be the number-one labor leader in Britain. He was not on Mr. Churchill's side and his presence in the Cabinet is variously regarded as the result of a Bevin ultimatum that Labor be represented in the war Cabinet or else—or as a shrewd move by the Conservatives to conciliate Labor. I do not know enough about either the Labor movement in Britain or British politics to give you an opinion on that.

But those who should know regard him as the most important man in Britain next to the Prime Minister, and many American observers and some English think he is the logical man to be Prime Minister at the end of the war. I found no difference of opinion in England on the score that he is an enormously powerful man, that "Labor" in England believes in him and follows him to a man, the extreme Left excepted. The extreme Left seems to feel that he is a very slick article. Nor is there any doubt that the attitude of British Labor toward the war changed sharply following his appointment to the Cabinet in May—and that since that time morale and production have improved enormously.

I saw Mr. Bevin about a week after I got to London.

I went by appointment to his office, past the usual sand-bagged and sentried barricade, and waited a few minutes in the bare hall outside his office. Most of the halls in most of the ministries in London are bare and charac-terized by sentries on duty and secretaries on the run. The visitor is made very conscious that there's a war on and that people are busy as hell. How they are in peace I don't know, but in war the Britishers are very punctual and I was rarely kept waiting as I made my rounds. The secretary brought me into Mr. Bevin's office, which was large and plain. We went right to it.

I told him that what interested a lot of Americans most was what kind of country the war was making of England. What was the position of Labor in the new world that was being born in the emergency—if a new world was being born? I said these things were of enor-mous interest to Americans because so many people at home were concerned lest Labor's position be sacrificed in our efforts to prepare ourselves for defense.

Mr. Bevin appeared to know exactly what he wanted to say in answer to these questions. He said: "I can tell you this. That England will never again tolerate large numbers of unemployed. England will never again tolerate the waste of skill that's gone on for so long. The big lesson of this war is that wealth is not land to walk over or money in the bank, but *skill*.

"And I can tell you this. That the profit motive will not and cannot solve the large problem of reconstruction in this country. The old capitalism is finished."

I asked him what he thought would take its place. He said, "Well now, look here. The first thing we've got to do is to win this war. And we are winning it. Things are humming now. As to what's coming after, we can't tell exactly, but I know what I want. I want to see all the large industries that serve the country nationalized.

"I have been trying to put it in words because I think it's one of the most important things to be done now. Or to be begun. If you don't mind, I'll give you copies of some speeches I've been making."

I asked him how much sacrifice he thought Labor had already made in the war effort—what standards had gone. I do not remember his exact answer, but it was to the effect that while the problem was complicated, Labor had not made any sacrifices at all in basic wages. The eight-hour day was still standard. In most of the war industries there was much overtime called for, but it was paid for at time and a half. So that while the worker had to work longer hours he was paid for them. He said, "There are many interesting things going on here. Take this Labor Ministry, for instance. I've worked out a whole new conception of a Labor Ministry's job. I don't see it my job to"—he used some phrase which I recall as meaning wet nurse. He said, "My Labor Ministry sees what Labor needs and then I put it up to other ministers to carry out the program. What kind of shelters do people who work want? I find out what they want and I tell the other ministers that's what they have to have. Now, that's quite a new kind of Labor Ministry."

Bevin is a good talker, with a clear, resonant voice and an easy, self-confident manner. He looks like his pictures. He leaned back in his chair while he talked and spoke rapidly. The notes I made of our conversation were made about an hour after I had left him.

I said to him, "Many people in America believe you will be the next Prime Minister. What do you think?" He smiled a broad, complacent smile and shook his head. He said, "No, no, no. Nothing like that. I just came here to do a job and I'm doing it and when it's done I will go back to my union." He said, "These fellows don't like me, you know. They don't approve of me." He was still smiling complacently.

He said, "In making a world that people like to live in you've got to do two difficult things. One is to organize it so that all the skill there is is used, and the other is to leave the individual man his freedom. Because the kind of a life that one man likes another man doesn't. You know, I always put it to them this way. You can't please Winston Churchill and the Archbishop of Canterbury with the same show." We both laughed.

He said, "I don't know whether I've been any help to you, but I'm glad to have seen you." We had been talking twenty or twenty-five minutes. When he took me to the door his secretary's office was filled with men carrying brief cases. One of them was saying impatiently to the secretary, "Well, you should have called me earlier." Another said, "Can't we go in now? Can't we go in now?" I left.

It's hard to have confidence in one's opinion after such a short talk with a man. On thinking over my talk with Mr. Bevin I was surprised that I felt it was exactly as I had anticipated it. I felt the man's vitality, his energy, his strength, his intelligence. I also felt that I had been with a very vain man and the modesty of his remark about going back to his union did not ring true.

After so much talk in America about Mr. Bevin's future and after my own feeling in talking with him that, whatever else, here was a man of stature, I was later to be surprised by how few people I met in London seemed seriously to consider Ernest Bevin as Prime Ministerial timber. The universal criticism was not of his ability, which everyone acknowledged, but of his "newness." The feeling was that he had not been long enough in public life. "Now, ten years from now, it's quite possible" was what most people said.

But I asked everyone who I thought might be interested who would be the next Prime Minister if anything should happen to Winston Churchill. Nobody had any idea. I felt that if I had to bet—certainly among such other Cabinet ministers as I met, I would certainly not bet on Ernest Bevin.

VISIT WITH CLAUDE COCKBURN

In America, the Communist Party is almost universally regarded as subversive. Many states barred its candidates in last November's election and most people believe that it either should or soon will be driven underground.

This is not at all the case in Great Britain, a nation already at war with a country with whom the Communist state of Russia is partially allied. The Communists' *Daily Worker* is sold on the streets—a boy hawks it outside the gates of the Ministry of Information every morning—and the leaders of the Communist Party agitate openly, organize mass meetings and demonstrations. I got hold of an editor of the *Daily Worker* to talk to him about it. He is Claude Cockburn, many years publisher of an often sensational news letter on international affairs called *The Week*—and once upon a time London correspondent for *Time* magazine. I knew him then—the son of the governor of a bank in Canada, Oxford graduate, and bright young man, when Lord Beaverbrook, then publisher of the *Daily Express* and now Minister for Aviation Production, was his most energetic admirer. I was told before I left America that he was probably in a concentration camp now. Nothing of the kind.

He talked to me for a long time and very frankly about conditions in England and the Communist Party's position.

He said the party was extremely unpopular with the government, but that it had decided rather than fight the war effort—it still felt the war an imperialist, capitalist, rather than an anti-Fascist one—it should concentrate its energies on a local issue. The issue it chose was improvement of shelters. He spoke bitterly and scornfully of the government's lack of interest in the way people were sheltered and very possessively about what shelter reform had already been achieved—this last in rebuttal to my statement that I had seen a good deal of evidence of effort at improvement. He said, "What improvement there has been is the result of our agitation."

He said, "The shelter problem's a terrific one. First we wanted to get them to open up the empty houses in the West End, but when the government did commandeer them, the owners boarded up the bathrooms and took out the fixtures and made slums of them. And then, the way they moved people didn't work out. They put families into a house in the West End and in the morning they'd get up and go out to buy their tea and bread for breakfast. And all they had to buy with were ha'pennies, and the West End shopkeepers had never even seen a ha'penny before. They were all very nice to them, but there wasn't anything they could sell them. And they were lonely and unhappy in strange surroundings, so they went back to the East End."

He said the Communist Party did organizing in the shelters and that the government didn't like that. He said, "Of course, what ought to be done is to move people in big unit groups so that their friends and families can be around them and things arranged so that they have the food they like to buy at prices they can afford."

He had many other ideas for improving shelters, most of which I thought intelligent. I remembered a government report I had read on morale which had listed as one of the problems the fact that the middle-class people in whose homes the poor were billeted complained that the government was imposing "the worst features of Communism and Fascism combined" on them. And that the poor people reported a not unnatural resentment at the hostility met in country billets.

What I found myself resenting in Cockburn's speech was that possessiveness I have referred to—a quality resulting from phrasing all his observations to suggest that his political party and his political party alone had any real interest in these things. I had seen too much evidence that this was nonsense.

The official Ministry of Home Security may or may not be working at maximum efficiency to improve shelters, but working, and working hard, they are. And so—more importantly—are the thousands of air-raid wardens and the millions of people who are themselves concerned, quite unconscious of politics. I felt Mr. Cockburn was perilously close to making "me too" his theme.

I asked Cockburn how the censors felt about the *Daily Worker*. He said, surprisingly, "They are pretty good. So far it really is a voluntary censorship. A paper doesn't have to submit anything to the censor it doesn't want. All the other papers have signed up voluntarily, but we just submit something about which we're in doubt. Of course, we are very careful to stay away from any military information, but the censorship doesn't bother us much. The only thing the government won't let us do is send the paper out of England."

He said the government's policy on mass meetings was not quite clear—that sometimes the men and women who passed out handbills announcing a meeting would be arrested and held for a while and at the same time the meetings they advertised would be unmolested.

I asked him what he thought about the position of Labor in the war effort—I asked him the same questions I had asked Bevin. He said, "Well, in the war industries, people earn a little more on account of the overtime. I would estimate that the cost of living had gone up twenty-five per cent, but many workers earn enough now to make that up and even more. It's hardest on the people who are not in war industries, who have to meet the increased cost of living on the same wages." He did not seem as interested in the Labor situation as in the shelter problem.

We were talking in my sitting room, just before the blackout, and there were half a dozen other people there —American and English journalists, an army officer, and an officer in the RAF. Cockburn and the journalists all knew each other and seemed on friendly terms. Later on they told me that the *Daily Worker* and the Communists were doing a good job of shelter work and that people respected them for it. They said the *Daily Worker's* horror stories of shelters were usually inaccurate or exaggerated—that they had checked up on a lot of them. They said that at the beginning the party had come out for the war effort, simply adding that democratic privileges and the position of Labor should not be sacrificed. And that at the time of the Nazi-Soviet pact they had switched, just the way the Communist Parties of other countries had switched all over the world. The man who had then been head of the party had disagreed and had wanted to go on supporting the war effort. They had thrown him out. The journalists guessed that although he was not the nominal head, Claude Cockburn was the most important man in the Communist Party in England now. They credited him with working out the new line—of simply skipping the war effort—of being neither against nor for it—and of trying to build up their membership by doing a good job with the local issue.

The conversation with Cockburn was one of those conversations with a political opponent that could be held only in England. The English who were there obviously disapproved of him. Yet they were interested in everything he said and listened to him and their praise of his work in the shelters was sincere and hearty.

I asked Cockburn what the Communist Party planned to do next. He said, "I think it's only a question of time before they lock us up." I was surprised, but Cockburn seemed very sure of his opinion. He said, "You will see. They can't let us go on working in the shelters because we are too effective and we show people how they can organize and get what they want. Herbert Morrison [Minister of Home Security, in charge of the shelters] has cracked down on us already. He got angry in Commons and said that all this shelter agitation was perilously close to Fifth Column work. That got him into a lot of hot water, because there were so many other people who weren't Communists who were working to improve the shelters and they all jumped on him. But he'll be back. I don't know when it will come, but we expect to be in jail soon."

It's not a very kind thing to say, but I had a feeling he was just a little disappointed that the party had not had harsher treatment already.

I asked about the Communists and their shelter effort in a great many places. I never found anybody very interested in the party or in Cockburn, which is probably a shame, because, as the English journalists pointed out, he is a very bright man and a lot of his ideas are very good.

CABINET

Among the members of the government with whom I talked in addition to Messrs. Churchill and Bevin were: Lord Beaverbrook; Herbert Morrison, Minister of Home Security, in charge of shelters; Duff Cooper, head of the Ministry of Information; Archibald Sinclair, Minister of Air; Messrs. Dalton and Cross, respectively Ministers for Economics and for Shipping; Lord Halifax, Foreign Minister and a holdover from Mr. Chamberlain's Cabinet; Viscount Cranborne, Minister for the Dominions; Sir John Reith, Minister for Reconstruction. I found every one of them interesting to talk to. Headlines on what they said:

Herbert Morrison said he did not believe in the big shelters and that he was trying to break up the existing ones, both for safety and health's sake.

Duff Cooper felt that the Americans in the Middle West were much more interested in the war than the Americans on the East Coast gave them credit for being.

Archibald Sinclair said that what the Air Ministry needed from America now was long-range bombers which could strike back at Germany—and which could be flown across from Canada under their own power.

Dalton, who is a Labor man, university educated, has the job of enforcing the blockade. (With the aid, of course, of the Navy.) He felt strongly about not feeding France, occupied or unoccupied. I agreed heartily with him that food for France this winter could not help but find its way into German stomachs.

Viscount Cranborne and Sir John Reith were most interested in public opinion in America. Both said they thought the U. S. would be more effective as an ally out of the war than in.

Lord Halifax talked to me about the spirit of sacrifice.

CAN OUR PLANES FIGHT?

I STARTED THIS report of my visit to England by saying that the most important news I brought back was of the significance of the battle of September 7 to 15—which was Hitler's first major defeat in eight years, and which history may yet regard as the turning point in the fortunes of Fascism.

But I might have led off with the almost equally startling news—to Americans—that the American fighter planes which we have sent to England are not fighting —and that I saw and heard completely convincing evidence that, as fighting machines, they cannot get in the same air with either the Messerschmidt 110 or 109, both of which are already practically obsolete and will soon be replaced by the German superfighter, the Messerschmidt 113. For which the British are more than prepared, but which will put the American fighting ships I saw in England another whole airplane generation further out of date.

The deficiency of the American pursuit plane is not primarily one of speed. It is a deficiency in offensive gun power. American planes are beautifully built, safe and easy to fly. But their characteristic armament is a battery of four machine guns, whereas both the Spitfires and the Hurricanes mount eight and the models which are about to succeed the Spitfires and the Hurricanes will mount twelve—or eight machine guns *plus* four cannon. There are other respects in which the best American fighters compare unfavorably with the fighters of the RAF and the *Luftwaffe,* but this is the principal one. The fighting power of a plane cannot easily be increased simply by sticking additional machine guns or cannon into it. The design of a fighting plane—which is after all nothing but a flying gun platform—must begin with its guns and the plane must be designed around them, the whole worked out to achieve the purpose of carrying the guns and their ammunition in the most effective manner.

The best American fighter planes already delivered to the British are used by them either as advanced trainers —or for fighting equally obsolete Italian planes in the Middle East. That is all they are good for.

Even the American RAF squadron—the Eagles—then training in England, which had planned to use American Brewster Buffalo fighters, had abandoned the idea and were being outfitted with Hurricanes.

I was going to lead off with this news—because I was very shocked by what I found out from the test pilots and engineers in England and what I saw at the station where the RAF tests its new models.

I did not do so because I wanted first to check what I had seen with American experts, to find out whether the situation was really as bad as it appeared or whether we really did have models which could compete with the best British and German fighters but which we were simply keeping to ourselves. And the situation seemed too serious to me to want to risk going off half cocked.

After the best check I have been able to make of models either in production or planned in this country —and after conferences with authorities on military strategy—the above statement still stands, but I have several important qualifications to make.

FIRST. As far as our own national defense goes, it is probably not necessary that we ever produce the best interceptor fighter in the world. Because the best interceptor fighter is a highly specialized plane necessary for defense only when the attacking bombers are themselves accompanied by fighter planes—a situation highly unlikely in the U. S. A., which would first have to be attacked by bombers flying such long distances that their protection by enemy fighters would be impractical. Our planes can shoot down unaccompanied bombers.

SECOND. Just as shock troops are at most a small percentage of any army, so the fastest and most lethal fighter planes are a small percentage of any air force. And if we have no aerial shock troops which can fight alongside the RAF against the *Luftwaffe,* the planes the British are getting from us are anything but useless—serve in dozens of other important capacities.

THIRD. There were American military observers in Great Britain when I was there. They are at last aware of the situation and they are now bringing back first-hand reports to guide and modify our own program.

And FOURTH, we have in manufacture in this country models which *probably* will be able to compete. I put this fact only fourth in my list of extenuating circumstances, because these newest American models will not be ready until late in the winter. They have not been tested in combat and if the history of the production of new models of airplanes teaches anything, it is that there are unforeseen imperfections and bugs in every new model which take time to be worked out. The German and English planes are not better because the German and English designers are smarter, but because their designs have been worked out and perfected under pressure and in actual combat.

But with all these qualifications, the fact still remains that the planes that Great Britain is producing for herself in British factories under a rain of German bombs must still stand alone between civilization and the *Luftwaffe*. To date we have been wholly unable to be of any assistance to England in the most crucial phase of the crucial fight for supremacy of the air over England.

In this chapter and a following one I will explain that the British are in business today solely by virtue of the superiority of the Hurricanes and Spitfires over the Messerschmidts. If the Hurricane and the Spitfire had not been able to defeat the Messerschmidt in combat over England, German bombers, instead of scattering bombs by night over Coventry in the dark, seeking to blow industrial needles out of residential haystacks, groping blindly and in general ineffectually for vital targets, would long since have been blackening the air over England by day, their dive bombers would have been picking off whatever they cared to pick off, and England would long since have become another Poland, bomb destroyed.

As long as the RAF fighter continues to lick the *Luftwaffe* fighting plane this cannot happen. But unless and until Americans can produce a fighting airplane the specifications of which I will presently describe, the RAF must go on relying on British-built planes. And in such a war as is being fought over England, it is not the British that need American help but the Americans that need British help—in manufacturing a fighting machine that can fight in the big league.

So much for American fighters. Now about American bombers. Any plane that can carry a large load a long way is useful as a bomber. For bombing at night it is not even necessary that the plane fly fast. But a first-class bomber is a bomber that not only can carry a large load of bombs to its objective, but one which can defend itself from attack by enemy planes. In this respect, the best American bombers now being produced still are as woefully deficient as the best American pursuit ships now in England.

This will not long be so, because we are now incorporating in our bomber designs defensive devices developed by the British. But it is true at present and the generalization goes not only for the flying fortresses but for every other American bombing plane, light and medium as well as heavy, now going to Britain.

The defensive device referred to is the automatic revolving machine-gun turret. It's not hard to understand the defensive superiority this turret gives. Every American has seen pictures of them—little glass cubicles housing a machine gunner and a battery of machine guns. Hydraulically operated, the turret itself swings in a 180-degree arc. And the guns can shoot from straight up to almost straight down. In other words, the turret can shoot its battery of guns in almost any direction.

The no-secret of the British bomber design is the wide tail of the fuselage, which permits the attachment of one of these turrets so that the gunner sits literally behind the whole plane and can protect it from any attack from the rear, from any direction, and from above and below. If you accept the desirability of this turret you will see at once the defect in the American design for defensive purposes. In converting the American Lockheed into a military ship, this turret must be stuck up in the middle of the back, an air-resisting bump on a log. And obviously it cannot protect the plane from attacks from the rear and below.

The standard English equipment on medium and light bombers is a turret in the nose and the tail. In the very largest bombers—even in our flying fortresses—there are additional turrets in the fuselage which retract like landing gear.

In bombing an undefended objective by night, defensive turrets are just so much waste load to carry. But already the Germans, as well as the English, have night fighters and the British bombers over Germany have so far had a remarkable record of success in shooting down attacking night fighters. The revolving turret has been an important reason for this success.

These are the highlights of the news on "how useful are our planes to the British?" No Britisher would make these statements as flatly as I have made them. First, because since they have developed their own fighters which can beat the *Luftwaffe*'s best, and are continuing to produce them in greater numbers despite what bombing the Germans can do by night, they do not feel an acute need for help from us in this department. Second, because they *do* need all kinds of other planes—trainers, reconnaissance planes and bombers, bombers, bombers—and they are getting these from us in increasing numbers and, as I have said, our bombers are now incorporating the British revolving turret in their design.

But to an American it is shocking news that we have at this date no planes that can fight in the front line in the battle for the defense of England—and that we have yet to prove that *any* of our models now planned or in production ever can compete. And it's impossible not to wonder what our American designers and manufacturers were doing through the years when the Hurricanes and the Spitfires and the Messerschmidts were being developed. If a hostile power with equipment as good as this could ever establish itself at a bombing base close enough to this continent to protect its bombers with fighters, there would be nothing we could do about it until we developed such a plane. And, to repeat, you cannot develop a major fighting machine overnight. The Hurricanes and Spitfires, the Messerschmidts and the still-newer British and German models have been developed by a long process of trial and error, gradual and constant improvement.

Since I have got back, many, many people have asked me: "What about our planes in England? Are they standing up? How do they compare?" I have written these conclusions before describing what I have seen at the fighter and bomber stations in England. War in the air is complicated and highly technical. As I have tried to say in setting down my qualifications to the flat statement that our best planes cannot compete with the best English and German planes, this sole fact is not the whole story. Firsthand descriptions of what I saw and heard in England follow. I think they will make both the indictment and its qualifications clearer to you.

Let's begin by visiting the front-line trenches of the air—the airport from which the interceptor squadrons take off, the fighter station.

I have been to half a dozen of them. They are like the airports we know at home only in that somewhere about there are flat fields or level runways from which the planes take off. In every other respect they are quite different. In the first place there are no hangars. Or if there are hangars they are empty. There are no control towers or machine shops visible. Nor as you come upon them are there any planes.

We reached the first over a rutted country road. A sentry stopped us at a barbed-wire and sandbagged barricade. I was with my friend, who is Wing Commander in the RAF. His job is in the coastal command and this was a fighter station. He had passes, showed them, and we went on. We passed some camouflaged shacks that seemed deserted. A soldier in fatigue uniform passed. We asked for the officers' mess or the adjutant's. He said if we went around beyond the shed we would see another shed in a hollow and the mess was in there. We found the shed he meant. Its doorway was protected by sandbags. We stepped into a room full of flying officers stand-ing about looking at bulletin boards, smoking and talk-ing. The British RAF uniform is a dusty blue with long trousers, and simply cut. Rank is recognized by the num-ber of bands of black piping at the lower end of the arms of the coat. It is the most modest uniform in the British Army.

We found the wing commander of the station in a neat little office behind a tidy desk. I was introduced. We shook hands and sat talking a few minutes. He had two squadrons up. He looked at his watch.

"One will be back in about twenty minutes. Nothing much going on," he said. "We put a couple of squadrons halfway up and let them cruise slowly to save fuel. They can stay up quite a long time that way and if anything happens they can get on up quickly."

The other squadrons were on the ground. I asked if I could walk around. He said: "Go on out. If you don't mind I have some reports to finish. I will pick you up and we will have lunch."

My friend, Wing Commander Gerald Maxwell, and I walked out and over a rise in the ground and along one side of what was obviously a runway. Not far beyond we came on the first plane suddenly. Its home was a sunken pit not much wider than its wings, sandbagged up on three sides six or eight feet high. In the center of the embankment that surrounded the plane a door opened down into a dugout. Gerald said the crew ducked down there when there was a raid. Several mechanics in coveralls were doing things to the plane. After the clip-pers and big flying boats and bombers I had seen, it was minute. Stand at one wing tip, take a few steps, and you bump the fuselage. The single wing is below and set well back toward the middle of the plane. The narrow motor seems to lean forward, away from the cockpit. Its three-blade metal propeller looks enormous. The pilot sits with a glass roof over him and the line of the plane from the back of his neck to the tail is straight and flat.

Gerald said: "That's how you can tell that it's a Spitfire. Hurricanes and Spitfires look almost exactly alike but in the Hurricane behind the pilot the back arches down to the tail in a curve."

There were no signs of guns on this Spitfire and I asked about that. Gerald took me to the leading edge of the wings and showed me strips of fabric three or four feet long, pasted along each.

"The guns are in there," he said. "You can never see them except just after they are fired. They paste the openings over to cut down wind resistance. The guns blow the fabric off when they are fired. There are four on each side. The Hurricane is a better gun platform than the Spitfire. These guns are set wider apart and they are more apt to move with the wing. You will see that the Hurricane's guns are tight together."

There was no other sign of life than the three mechanics who did not seem to have anything very urgent to do and paid no attention to us. We walked on down the edge of the field. Again tucked away out of sight we came upon another plane bay. In this one a house seemed to have been built around the Spitfire's nose. Gerald said they were taking the motor apart inside it and that that kept the servicing operation dry and warm. We walked past half a dozen other planes, each in its own bay, some apparently ready, some partially dismantled.

Suddenly the air above us began to hum. I had been in England long enough so that humming air made me nervous and then I remembered it must be the squadron coming in. We could hear them circle the field above low clouds, and off to the right they came through, broke formation, turned the length of the field one by one, banking sharply, and landed on another runway, out of sight. Gerald looked at the empty field. We could see only two or three plane bays. He said: "That is called dispersal. Dispersal is a big word in this war. Everything has to be dispersed so that not much of it can be hit at a time. It is not as hard as you think. It works very well.

"The German dispersal is excellent," he added as an afterthought.

He should have known, since his job is to photograph it.

We had lunch at the officers' mess which was served by waitresses. The butter and the sugar didn't seem to be rationed. The food wasn't as well cooked as in London. The atmosphere was sober, casual. If you have read of how the fighter squadrons lived in the last war you would not have recognized this scene. The British fighter pilots I met are quite serious young men.

On another fighter field we visited, the ships were not in bays but simply stood here and there behind and beyond gently rolling hills. Gerald's brother's squadron was here and we were directed to his hut on the far side of the field, quite a long walk from the headquarters. It was a galvanized-iron hut about fifteen feet long with an arched roof and it had a sofa and some chairs and a table and a monkey in it. Two pilots had bought the monkey over a week end in London. They were afraid it would catch cold so they had an electric heater propped on a chair pointed at it.

There were fifteen or twenty pilots in this little room and they all got up and stood when we came in, because Gerald is a Wing Commander. They filled the room until you could hardly see it or them. Their costumes were identical. On their feet were heavy flying boots and around their chests and backs they wore bright-yellow life preservers which bunched into funny shapes. They call the life preservers "Mae West" and they must always wear them. Their parachutes were in the seats of their planes and their helmets with their earphones and oxygen masks hung on the sticks of their ships. They were ready as they stood in flying boots and "Mae Wests" to run out onto the field and climb into their machines at any minute.

While we were making awkward conversation, the motors outside suddenly began to go. They made me jump. But no one moved and one of them saw that I was confused. He said: "They watch the thermostats and when the motors get cool they warm them up again. You see they always have to be kept warmed up."

Before we left the hut the motors had been turned off again.

I thought, "These are the young men who fight the *Luftwaffe* every day. They are on duty now. If the gong outside rings they will rush past me and go out to kill or be killed."

They decided the monkey was a good subject to talk to me about and I heard a great deal about its diet and its disposition. I felt very awkward talking with the men who were fighting every day because I don't think one can help but feel awkward with men who are doing your fighting for you while you are safe on the ground going about your business. I could only talk to them about their trade when I talked with one or two alone, in a private house or a restaurant. I tried to get a picture of what they had been doing before we came in. A couple must have been reading dog-eared detective stories. The books were turned face down, opened. We had interrupted a game of darts and a card game in which four or five were playing. Hung on the wall in one corner was a board with names painted on it. I went over to read it. The names were of members of the squadron who had been decorated and the decorations and the dates were listed. It went back to 1915. Second name on the list was my friend Gerald Maxwell's. I pointed it out to him and he was embarrassed. He said: "Yes, this is Squadron 56. It was Ball's squadron first and then I had it. Its record was over four hundred planes in the last war."

He said it was flying Hurricanes now and asked me if I would like to see one. The squadron leader came out with us to show us around.

A few feet from the hut there was a plane with its tail jacked up into the air. It faced a bit away, its nose pointed down into a pit about twenty-five yards ahead. The squadron leader said: "There's where we test the guns. They're fitting a squadron with cannon there now."

We stopped and looked. An airplane cannon is really an overgrown machine gun. Its shell is almost as big across as a quarter. The shell is six or eight inches long. It's vicious-looking, and now I could see how the gun was fitted into the wing because the fabric was off, and I could also see how the magazine fed it its shells. The machine guns in an airplane's wing can fire only for eight seconds continuously. Eight seconds, not eight minutes. But this may be as many as sixteen bursts of fire. All the machine guns—or all the cannon—fire at once. If the plane mounts both, there are two triggers, one for each. Since the guns are below the center of gravity of the plane their recoil pulls the nose down. The group leader said: "You don't feel the machine guns much, but the cannon give you a little jolt."

We walked on over to a Hurricane. I could see the difference between its lines and the Spitfire's. By invitation I got into the cockpit. The seat can be lowered or raised so that the pilot is sitting up high with his head well into the glass roof which the pilots call the greenhouse—or he can drop himself out of sight into the plane. The squadron leader climbed up on the wing and was explaining it. He turned on a switch and there suddenly appeared on the windshield in front of me a ring of light, perhaps six inches in diameter, with a cross light in the middle.

"That's the sight," he said. "Good, isn't it? Works by mirrors."

There are three controls in an airplane: a rudder to steer it by horizontally, which one works with one's feet; flippers in the tail, which steer the nose up or down and are manipulated by pushing a stick forward or back; and the ailerons in the wing tips, which bank the plane. In some ships aileron controls are attached to the stick so that it is simply moved from side to side to move the ailerons. In others—in the big commercial ships, for instance—the ailerons are moved by a wheel that is attached to the stick. The old fighting ships used to have a simple stick control. The Hurricane has a combination of the two. Instead of a wheel, the stick breaks just above the pilot's knees, and the ailerons are controlled by moving the top part of it from the left to right.

The group leader said the Messerschmidts still use a straight stick, that he thought the Hurricane's controls were better because you didn't bump your knees when throwing it into a sharp bank. On the top of the stick, where a knob would be on a gear shift, it had a small ring, a little bigger than the ring you could make with your thumb and forefinger. This is what the pilot holds on to while he flies the ship. There is a large button set into this ring the top of it just about where your thumb falls when you reach for the ring naturally. I reached for the ring and the group commander said: "Just a minute, sir. You know it's loaded. I think the safety's on but may I look?"

The safety catch, which went on by turning the whole button, was on.

"The guns are always loaded," he said again.

The instrument panel was very complete. I examined the helmet. Earphones were set into the flaps and there was a muzzle in the front like a gas mask's through which the pilot breathed oxygen. All the fighting in high altitudes is done with the pilot breathing oxygen. They might not like oxygen, but if they did not have it they would not be able to shoot straight. They tested this out on the ground in the decompression chamber and found it true. There was a circular mirror fastened over the top of the windshield, but the pilot said it wasn't much use and that the ships were very blind from the rear.

Because of this blindness, when the fighters are in formation they always fly with at least one plane above and behind as a rear guard. It weaves back and forth, twisting to look in every direction. The plane that does this weaving and watching is called "Tail-Ass-Charlie." People watching a British squadron fly across the sky have been known to get excited and think they see it being pursued by a German plane maneuvering for a gun shot. But that is simply "Tail-Ass-Charlie." Pilots say it is very wearing because you have to keep throwing yourself back and forth across the rear of the formation at 300 or 350 miles an hour. Also, it is dangerous because if a Messerschmidt is out of your sight above you and sees your squadron he will dive on the rear to finish off "Tail-Ass-Charlie" first.

I spent a long time looking at the Hurricane, examining its workmanship. I fly a little myself and I have been around airplanes and airports a great deal. I had never seen a plane as well and compactly and strongly built as this. When I remarked on it both Gerald and the group commander, who was showing it to us, told me stories about things that had happened to Hurricanes and Spitfires in the air—things that would have put down any other plane at once and yet the pilots were able to fly them back to the home field—half of the tail shot off by cannon and controls partially out, etc. Gerald said: "You should see the way a squadron comes back from a real fight. The ships often come back coughing and spitting, their motors plastered, wings and fuselage full of holes."

I asked what the difference was between a Huricane and a Spitfire—fighting wise. I found out that the Hurricane was more maneuverable, fights best around 20,000 feet. The Spitfire goes both higher and faster, but is not quite so handy in a dogfight.

"If you can," they told me, "you put your Spitfires at 30,000 feet and your Huricanes at 20,000 and then everything's perfect. The Spitfires knock them down and the Hurricanes chew them up."

Here for the first time I heard what I was to hear again and again wherever I went—that the morale of the German fighters had turned definitely bad in the last month. The Messerschmidts will no longer stay and fight. What they try to do now is to come over very high and, spotting an English plane, go for it in one long steep dive. Get in a single burst. Continue the dive. Swoop out of it and go home. The English pilots do not like this, because in the first place it means that they rarely get a crack at the Messerschmidt and in the second, because when the Germans, who don't get many planes, do get on the back of one there is nothing he can do about it because the German has come down out of the sun and from behind and so fast that the English pilot does not see him until it's too late. And the burst is in and either cripples his plane or does not cripple it— and there is the German—away into the distance.

Up until the Italian planes came over, losses on both sides had been very low for a month. This is why. There has been no mass flying by the Germans by day. No dog-fighting. When there is dogfighting the Spitfires and the Hurricanes have it all over the Messerschmidts, partly because they can maneuver better but principally because they have eight guns to the Messerschmidt's four, so that burst for burst the chances of downing the German are two to one in the Briton's favor.

Moreover, they tell me the Messerschmidts have at least one bad flying habit. When they are in a steep dive their aileron controls lock, which means they cannot turn from one side to the other. They can only get out of their dive by pulling their nose up in a straight line. And it takes them several thousand feet to do that. So that if an English fighter sees a Messerschmidt dive on him and can get out of the way and get up speed himself, the Messerschmidt it utterly helpless. The Hun sits there, a pilot told me, tugging at his controls but nothing happens. Wind is going by his ailerons so fast they can't be moved. Even in a Hurricane or a Spitfire it takes a lot of strength to turn one over in a dive.

It was the next day that I saw my first Messerschmidt 109. Alongside the Hurricanes and Spitfires, they are easy to tell apart. The wing tips of the English ships are tapered and the tips of the German wings are squared, giving them a sawed-off effect.

I am sorry to disillusion a great many Americans, but I found the captured Messerschmidt extremely well equipped with instruments. I talked with many officers about this and each told me there was nothing to the legend that only the squadron leader in a German squadron had flying instruments.

The plane itself did not seem to me quite as substantially built as the English planes, but the margin of difference was narrow. The idea that German fighter planes are jerry-built is of course nonsense. You cannot fly a jerry-built ship at 300 or 400 miles an hour, using it as a gun platform for machine guns.

Studying the design of the Messerschmidt, for what it's worth, the tail assembly seemed to me obsolete. It used the same mechanics for trimming the ship that I had in a little sport Fairchild. The whole tail surface moves up and down. In all modern ships, both in England and America, fore and aft stability is adjusted by small tabs on the flippers.

The stick in the German cockpit is very short, must hardly reach above the pilot's knees. Its handle is like the emergency brake handle in an American car. The button you press in at the top of an American emergency brake lever is the button that turns on the machine guns in the Messerschmidt.

Also a fiction is the story that the German pilots are reckless lads in their teens. I talked with the head of the Air Corps Intelligence, one of whose jobs it is to keep track of such things, and he told me the German pilots were rarely younger than twenty, more often nearer twenty-five. He said only two that had been captured so far had been trained since the war began. Wherever the new pilots the Germans are training are being used, it is not over England.

The operation of fighting in the air does not begin with the clumsily muffled young men running across the airport to get into the cockpits of their pursuit ships. The process of fighting in the air begins on a drafting board with a design for a fighting machine. A fighting machine is only secondarily an airplane. It is primarily a gun platform—in simpler language: a place from which guns are fired. As a fighter it is meaningless that an airplane is fast or economical or maneuverable or that it can climb rapidly or dive steeply, if after it has got to the scene of its encounter with an enemy plane it cannot shoot it down before it's shot down.

There are a number of other deficiencies in the American machine as a fighting weapon but this is the principal one. A Messerschmidt 109 has only four machine guns. The fact that the English pursuit ships have eight is the reason why the British won the battle of September 7 to 15, although the odds in number of ships were overwhelmingly against them. The other faults with the American pursuit ships as fighting machines are these:

They tend to armor inadequately the pilot. The pilot should have armor at least under his seat and behind his back—armor strong enough to protect him from machine-gun fire. Some of the German planes armor the top of their pilot's head and the back of his neck and the calves of his legs also. There have been occasions when as many as three Spitfires emptied their full loads —twenty-four machine guns in all—into the back of a German pilot without succeeding in killing him.

The American pursuit planes are definitely too compli-cated to fly off the ground into combat. I have had pur-suit pilots estimate that it took them as long as twenty minutes to adjust their American machines for combat after taking off. Wheels must come up. Gasoline tanks must be opened and closed. Manifold pressures and pro-peller pitches must be regulated. In the cockpits of some of the U. S. pursuit ships there are lists of things to do taking off and landing, facing the pilot where he sits so that he won't forget. The Hurricane and the Spitfire have few adjustments. Flaps and wheels work automati-cally on the pressure of buttons. There is a simple, single booster (supercharger) control on the motor. This differ-ence is enormously important for two reasons.

First, the pursuit ship may have to go into action within a few minutes after getting off the ground. The Spitfires and the Hurricanes had to in the early days of the war when dive bombers came over to Dover.

But second and more important, complicated controls in pursuit cockpits completely fail to understand matériel with which the fighting is done. The matériel is a young man in a hell of a hurry, probably in a highly emotional state. The matériel is not a commercial pilot with a long run ahead of him and gasoline to conserve, with per-formance charts to fill out and hand in to the operations manager. He only wants one thing of his motor: all the power it can give him as quickly as it can give it.

The above statements are carefully made after being on the field. I spent a day at the experimental station where all kinds and varieties of ships are tried out. I did not see the American Airacobra which had not reached the field. But I did see the Brewster (Buffalo) fighter and others. The most elementary check was completely convincing: these machines cannot compete with either the existing English or German fighters. (The English experimental field had Messerschmidts there as well.)

The many, many English pilots I talked to were friendly and hesitant in their criticism. But very definite. There is obviously no question but that if these ships were of use to them they would be in the air. The man who fights for his life in the air has no pride of authorship in who builds his plane. We in this country have some immediate and serious thinking to do on this score.

There is no question but that this thinking will be healthy only if it follows these lines:

Our thinking must acknowledge the fact that the RAF knows more about fighting than we do. That their opinion is not something to be resisted, but something to be sought and courted. That we have to gain the time we have already lost. That the way to do this is to acknowledge the experience of the most experienced fighting men. We must take their advice. We must set up a minimum standard of performance and spend no time or energy or money making fighter ships that will not live up to it.

This was obvious to me before I had spent a day looking the scene over. From then on I always put my questions in this form: "What is the minimum performance of a fighter that will be able to compete with the *Luftwaffe* next spring?"

This is a composite picture: the plane must be able to

fly at 400 miles an hour. It must be highly maneuverable and the controls must not lock in a dive. It must be able to fight at altitudes of between 30,000 and 35,000 feet— six and seven miles in the air. It must be simple, almost automatic, to get off the ground and into trim for fighting. The pilot must be armored as well as his opponent— back of the neck, back of the seat, back of the legs. It must be a sound gun platform for twelve machine guns or six cannon or four cannon and six machine guns. Or some such combination of both.

TAIL-ASS-CHARLIE

SLANG

1940's RAF has yet to produce a slang as rich as 1918's. These were all I could gather:

On the ground antiaircraft fire is called.........ack-ack

In the air pursuit pilots call it....................flak
(Said to be an abbreviation for a German word.)

When it breaks around bombers they call it.......mud

To be attacked in the air is to be..............blitzed

A German plane is...........................a bandit

To be killed or destroyed...................written off

Lively doings are called.......................a flap
(When many planes fight in the air there is said to be a "flap on.")

But to lose one's head, to get in a dither, is to..get a flap on

To be bored is to be.....................browned off

A yellow or inflated life preserver which all pilots wear is called...............................a Mae West

A pilot who flies to the rear and above a flying squadron, weaving from side to side to watch enemy aircraft is called...........................Tail-Ass-Charlie

The explosion of a bomb is usually called.......a bang

A burst of machine-gun fire, either outgoing or incoming..a squirt

The pilot's cockpit...................the greenhouse

Typical use: "I gave him a squirt in the greenhouse and wrote him off."

The American word stooge is in vogue, meaning just what it means here.

THIS IS the story of a twenty-two-year-old pilot who is now flying a Hurricane pursuit ship in a squadron stationed close to London.

I have chosen it to write—amongst many that I've heard firsthand—because it's the story of a young man who is *not* regarded as a hero. He has never broken up a formation of bombers single-handed, nor has he taken off alone, intercepted a fleet of Messerschmidts, downed two, and chased the rest home—as had two of the men I met who had recently been decorated. I shall not call my undecorated hero by his name, because he is very shy and this story will embarrass him enough as it is. I shall call him Lieutenant Harte, and this is his story in as much detail as I can remember.

When the war began he was in Oxford and had done a little flying there under the direction of the RAF. (Before the war the RAF subsidized and supervised the training of such students in the university as cared for flying.) He went to France shortly after the war began, flying a Spitfire.

The first time he was shot down was over Belgium, during the retreat. He was in a dogfight with a Messerschmidt 109 at 28,000 or 29,000 feet, breathing oxygen through his mask, watching the German as the two planes circled, sparring for an opening.

The first thing he remembers is getting what felt like a terrific kick in the seat of his pants. His plane went several hundred feet straight up in the air. He said he couldn't imagine what had happened to him. It wasn't the Messerschmidt, which he had been watching at the time, and he was well in over his own lines.

Then, within a few seconds, he got another kick in the pants, the plane went on up four or five hundred feet and this time, he says, when he looked out of the greenhouse his plane didn't have any wings on it. He says he said to himself, "I don't know what did it, but it's obviously time to get out." Then he thought, "Only flaks (anti-aircraft fire) could have done that, but I still don't understand it because I'm not over enemy territory." By this time he found himself and his fuselage upside down. The glass cover to the cockpit of a Spitfire slides back. He was looking down through the closed glass cover to the ground below him. Using both hands, he got the glass hatch free and slid it clear. Then, he says, he expected to fall out and he wanted to fall out, but he didn't because he'd forgotten all about his safety belt. What was left of the plane continued to fall, upside down. Finally he remembered the safety belt and he let go the clasp. He dropped out sharply and the wind began to turn him around. As he turned, his arms flew out from his sides and he found himself looking at his hands. He says that when he saw his hands he thought very clearly that he didn't like them because they ought to be pulling the rip cord on his parachute, and they weren't. He said he thought to himself, "Harte, you're the damnedest fool there ever was, because why did you undo your safety belt before you got your hand on your rip cord?" He said it seemed a long time later that he realized he was thinking nonsense. In a kind of rush of panic, he looked for the handle of the rip cord, found it, and pulled.

He said that while he was pulling he thought, "Now don't worry. It will be some time before the parachute opens." But the parachute opened instantly and seemed to jerry him around in an upright position before he had finished the gesture of pulling the cord.

All these little details he remembered with great clarity.

He says that after the parachute had opened he found himself sitting there with no sense of motion. He felt "very safe and sound" and decided that this was rather a unique opportunity to look around at the countryside. He says he was still very high up. As he looked down, the first thing that he noticed was that something was happening directly beneath him. He could see the puffs of cannon firing and noticed that men were running across a clearing. He says this made the landscape even more interesting and he tried to make some sense out of the battle that was going on underneath him and to figure out who was on whose side and was trying to do what. Then as he dropped lower, things began whizzing by him and he said to himself, "This would be my luck. To bail out in the middle of a battle and get shot by a stray bullet."

The lower he got the closer the bullets came until—he thinks he must have been about a mile high then—it came to him that this was no battle going on beneath him, the shooting he was observing was at him. Machine guns, rifles, and an antiaircraft battery were all shooting at him. He said, "Then I really got scared." He came down the last few thousand feet knowing that things were very wrong and that the shooting was coming from people on his own side. He landed in a field, picked himself up, yelling at the top of his lungs, *"Je suis anglais, je suis anglais."* ("I am English, I am English.")

He was in Belgium, all right. Belgian soldiers ran up all around him, pointing their guns at him. But they didn't fire and finally an officer came. And when the officer recognized his uniform he told the men to put down their rifles and came up and embraced young Mr. Harte.

The officer turned out to be a count, a cousin of the King of Belgium, and he took Harte back to headquarters in his car, to arrange to have him sent on to the English lines. When the time came for him to go, the Belgian count who was the cousin of the King said, "I would much appreciate it if you would give me a souvenir of this occasion. Perhaps your parachute?" Harte said he didn't think he could give him his parachute because parachutes were expensive and they would want him to bring it back.

The count said, "Your helmet, possibly?" Harte, who is of good Scotch stock, said, "Good heavens, no. I have to buy my own helmet."

So they settled on his pipe.

So he asked the count who was a cousin of the King of Belgium why it was he wanted a souvenir. And the count said, "I don't think you understand. I'm in command of the antiaircraft battery. Yours is the first plane my battery has ever shot down. It is a very special occasion."

Lieutenant Harte thought it was a little too special.

All of this story Lieutenant Harte remembered in great detail, since it was his baptism to fire—and because of the count who was the cousin of the King of Belgium. His later adventures he took much more casually.

After the Belgian episode Lieutenant Harte was ordered back to England to get himself another plane. Dunkirk was very close now. He and some other officers went across the Channel on a foggy night in a trawler. When they were well off the French coast they were hailed in the dark by an English voice. It asked who they were. Since it was an English voice, they replied honestly. But the English voice turned out to be coming from a German torpedo motorboat and it was followed by machine-gun fire. They couldn't see the German boat in the dark and the fog, even though it turned on a searchlight shortly after it began to shoot. A gun crew on the trawler shot back at the searchlight.

The sequence of events here is confused in my memory. I recall that Harte's trawler was sunk by a torpedo and that he was picked up by another and brought on across the Channel, but whether the first German torpedo boat sunk him or whether he got away from this one and was sunk by another, I forget.

By the time he got back to England and rejoined his squadron, Dunkirk was over. He began to fly Hurricanes, which he liked better than Spitfires. His next two incidents were not so dramatic as the first. He was simply shot down twice and both times flew his Hurricane to land on English soil. Once he was fighting over the Channel and once over the Thames estuary. On neither occasion did he know where the bullet came from that disabled his plane. He was simply flying along and all of a sudden his motor was hot and things began to go wrong. The first time he had a choice as to whether to make a landing in enemy territory or try to get home. He decided to try to get home. He knew the motor was hit in some vital point because the temperature began to rise, but that was all. The temperature kept on rising all the way home. When he was over England, but before he had found his field, the cooling fluid caught fire.

Fire in the air, nowadays, comes not from explosions in the gas tank, but from the cooling fluid. Gas tanks on Hurricanes and Spitfires are what is called bulletproof. Bulletproof does not mean what it sounds like, for machine-gun bullets puncture gas tanks quite easily. What it means is that the insides of the tanks are coated with a chemical substance that closes the hole made by the bullet after the bullet has passed through, so that the tank will not leak. It does not catch fire even from an incendiary bullet, because there is so little oxygen inside the tank. What catches fire is the inflammable cooling fluid which becomes explosive if overheated. Even if it doesn't catch fire its fumes, when overheated, are often deadly.

Lieutenant Harte's ship had been hit in the radiator. The cooling fluid leaked out. The motor overheated. The cooling fluid finally caught fire. He came swirling into his airport with smoke and flames all around him.

The next time it happened was very like that last, except that Lieutenant Harte now had had some experience with cooling fluid catching fire, and after his motor reached a certain temperature he shut it off. The motor immediately froze. There was no airport in sight, so he came down in a field. Landing a fast pursuit ship in a farmer's field with a dead stick is no fun. You have to pick your field in a hurry and do the best you can with it. The field that Harte picked out when he was 5000 feet high did not look so good when he was only a few hundred feet up. He says "it obviously wouldn't do." At the far end of the field there was a farmer's house. By the time he had finally decided on the unsuitability of the field, the top of the farmer's house was higher than he was, so that he had to use the last of his speed to get up and over it, to get to what he hoped was a better field on the far side. Somewhere in the air just beyond the farmer's house the Hurricane stopped flying. It went into the ground nose first at something over a hundred miles an hour. The nose with the motor in it broke off and Harte and the rest of the plane went on across the field. He was not hurt. He does not consider this much of an incident except that he did think it *was* rather extraordinary the way the motor broke off and saved his life by doing it.

He admitted that the next time he was shot down it might make a story. That time—his fourth—he was functioning as "Tail-Ass-Charlie" for a squadron of Hurricanes and they were flying over enemy territory, going down along the German-held coast of France. "Tail-Ass-

Charlie," as I have explained before, is what they call the pilot who flies above and behind a squadron of pursuit planes and weaves back and forth in figure eights to protect the squadron's rear. It is, as Harte explained, a nasty job, because "Tail-Ass-Charlie" has to fly so fast and to throw himself into such violent and continuous banking that he is either continually blacking out—that is, throwing the blood out of his head until he goes temporarily blind—or coming close to it. In fact, the trick is to keep as close to it as possible without actually losing your sight from lack of blood. He said he was doing quite nicely, except it was late afternoon and they were flying east and the sun was right up behind him. Two Messerschmidts with cannon came out of this sun and were on his tail before he could do anything about it. As they dived they made a "V" about forty-five degrees wide, converging on the back of his neck. Both of them let go from very close, crossed and went under him and disappeared. Two shells from one and one shell from the other hit his Hurricane in the tail assembly.

Now, a single twenty-millimeter cannon shell is theoretically lethal to any plane it hits, wherever it hits it. That is, even a big two-motor bomber is supposed to be vulnerable to a single cannon-shell explosion, wherever it happens, because the explosion breaks the ribs of the plane. The three cannon shells that hit Harte's Hurricane tore off not quite half the covering of the horizontal tail and the flippers and part of the vertical stabilizer fin and part of the rudder.

Harte explained this to me in detail because he was trying to impress on me how much punishment a Hurricane can take and still fly home. It never occurred to him until much later in his story to throw in the casual fact that the three cannon-shell explosions had given him a shower bath of steel fragments from the rear. The back of his head, his neck and his back were protected by armor plate, off which most of the shell fragments bounced. Fifty some odd pieces of steel shell fragment were not stopped by armor plate, came through the bottom of his seat, and lacerated his legs as if by a discharge of buckshot a few feet away. It literally never occurred to him to tell me this part of the story until I asked him how he signaled to the English bombers.

This is how he got to the English bombers to begin with. After the cannon shells had hit him he sat up over the German coast a minute and felt his controls. The plane still seemed to be able to fly. The squadron whose rear he had been protecting disappeared within a few seconds. They probably didn't know he had been hit. Once again, he had the choice of landing safely in enemy territory or of trying to get his plane back to England. He decided he'd try to take it back. He knew when he turned the nose of his plane toward Dover that the best he could hope for was to land on his own soil. If any kind of German plane met him on the way home he would be utterly unable to defend himself. He could barely stay in the air, losing altitude all the time. But still he decided he would take what was left of his plane home. He turned north.

Halfway across the Channel he caught up with three British Bristol-Blenheim bombers, returning from a daylight raid. He recognized them as English and he said they looked awfully good to him. They were his chance of protection until he could land his ship on English soil. He flew down to come alongside them. When he got there —they were in formation—instead of welcoming smiles he watched six gun turrets swing around and twelve machine guns train on him. Harte said to me, "There's one thing that bombers hate more than anything else in the world and that's a pursuit plane. Friend or foe, they just don't like us." I said, "Why?" and he said, "Because sometimes pursuit planes get mixed up and shoot at their own bombers." He also thought it possible that what with this and that they had first mistaken him for a German. He said he began to feel pretty desperate and lonely and he couldn't think how to make the bombers understand what he wanted, which was simply protection until he could get back to England. He said they finally saw that he was not an enemy plane and that when they did, instead of moving their guns off him, all the gunners began waving him off, telling him to go somewhere else. Finally he had an idea. He took a handkerchief out of his pocket, reached down and dipped it in the blood from the wounds on his feet and held the bloody handkerchief out over his head. As I listened to the story, this was the first I heard of his having been wounded.

He was very pleased with his ingenuity. He said the bombers caught on at once—the minute they saw the bloody handkerchief. "But then," he said, "they scared me even more, because they got so curious all the crews began crowding into the gun turrets to look at me, and I was afraid they would veer over and bump into me, because I couldn't steer very well.

"But," he added, "I finally had them, you know. I just cut down in front of them and kept them right up on my tail. They still couldn't go quite as fast as I and when I had them up on my tail I knew that if any trouble came they would catch it first." He said this as if he had played a rather sly trick on the bombers—a sly and not entirely cricket trick.

This time he didn't try for a forced landing in a field, but when he got to England left the bombers and flew straight to his home airport. He didn't know why he did this, except that he had a strong desire not to land anyplace new, but to go home.

His landing must have been spectacular. The technique of landing a plane is to slow up first and when you are close to stalling speed and close to the ground at the same time to pull the stick back, as if braking with the tail. Hurricanes are fine flying ships and with the flaps down they land around 60 miles an hour.

Having now practically no skin on his tail surface, Harte had to come in at around 160 miles an hour with the stick as far forward as it would go, to keep the denuded tail from smacking the earth. He says he used the whole airport in a great swirl of dust. Then he taxied over to his plane station, where the mechanics were waiting. The head mechanic came out to him and stood a few feet from the plane, looking it over. His remark was, "Well, Lieutenant, you've done a proper job now. No work for me, thank you kindly. This is a factory job." That was all.

They have since got most of the fifty-odd pieces of shell fragment out of the Lieutenant's legs, but there are quite a few that weren't worth going after still there.

As you do, hearing stories like this, I looked down at his feet while he was talking. He had on his flying boots and I noticed for the first time that inside of the right heel there was a deep groove in the leather about four inches long. He saw me looking at it and he said, "Yes, that was from that time, but they really didn't hurt the boots, you know. They are quite all right and it's rather nice to have a scar like that, isn't it?"

The fifth time Lieutenant Harte got shot down—or am I boring you? Lieutenant Harte was sure he was boring me when I insisted on his telling me—he got his plane back to England but lost it because the only place he could find to land after his motor had been shot out over the Channel was along the beach on the south coast, and although he got the plane down quite whole, it was outside the barbed-wire entanglements and the mined landing areas. He said, "The engineers have done a lot of work on thinking how to get that plane out, but they haven't been able to solve the problem and it is still sitting there on the beach."

He said, "It's really quite appalling, you know, the money I've cost the government with all those planes. It wouldn't be quite as bad if they could get that one on the beach back."

The sixth time he was shot down Lieutenant Harte said was really not worth talking about because "absolutely nothing happened," and by this time I had been at him for an hour and he was getting really shy talking about himself.

In this whole narrative of his experiences, which I had insisted on and he had given me because I wanted it so much, I suddenly realized he had not told me a single story of victory—a single incident which directly reflected credit on him or made him a hero. He permitted himself to tell me about the times he had been shot down because those were stories on him, and it certainly never occurred to him that there was anything heroic about his bringing in damaged planes when he could have saved his skin any time by landing in enemy territory and saying good-by to the war. Or by jumping out in his parachute again.

Not from him, but from others in his squadron, I learned that he had four confirmed planes to his credit, one of them a bomber, and that he had probably shot down as many more that were not confirmed. I saw him once again, and this time I reproached him for not telling me at least about the bomber. This is what he said: "Oh, the bomber was absolutely nothing. It was on its way home and I got a good shot at it. And it went down quite near the field. It was really absolutely nothing."

To shoot down a bomber you've got to come in through the bomber's defensive gun fire, probably kill its rear gunner from a range of 200 yards, keep on coming in over or under the bomber until you can get its pilot or one of its motors. Planes are hit from farther off, but a pilot is a good pilot only when he has the courage and determination to come in to very close range—which is why morale is so important in the air.

To change the subject, Harte went on about the bomber and said, "They were talking about it in the pub when I stopped in that evening for a glass of beer. It was rather unpleasant, you know, because someone told them I had got it." I said, "What did they *do* in the pub?" He said, "Oh, but they got so bloodthirsty, you know. They all clamored around me and said they hoped all the crew had been killed when it crashed. It was very unpleasant, you know. Some of those German pilots are awfully good, you know. And besides you don't think of an enemy plane as being anything but an enemy plane— something to shoot down. My, they were bloodthirsty beggars in that pub."

XII

TECHNIQUE OF MURDER

THE MOST immediate question of most immediate importance to civilization—and I am measuring my words—is who is winning the battle between the RAF and Adolf Hitler's *Luftwaffe*.

There are other pressing questions. The war under the sea and on the surface of the sea, which has had the least publicity, may in the end be the most consequential.

The progress of the social revolution in England, the breaking down of its hard class consciousness into the classlessness of a true democracy overshadows our future and our children's future.

But if the RAF cannot withstand the *Luftwaffe,* then it does not matter how many ships the submarines sink or do not sink. And we will never have a chance to know whether the bomb-inspired social revolution in England will fulfill itself by creating a new and better society.

I have written about bomb damage in England and said that you cannot understand it until you have acquired some sophistication in what the word "bombed" means—it can mean so many different things. Likewise, you cannot understand the tide of the war in the air without having at least an elementary technical understanding of what is a wholly technical method of killing.

First, the objective of the war in the air over Britain is control of the air itself. Once an invader has control of the air and can do what he likes in it, he has won the war in the air. For example, the war in the air over Britain bears no resemblance to the war in the air over Finland or Poland or Holland or Belgium or France. Because over Britain the invaders have not got control of the air. This is a definite statement which I will proceed to prove. Over Finland the Russians had control of the air, in sheer weight of numbers of planes flying. No matter how brilliantly they muffed on the ground it was only a matter of so many weeks before the Russian bombers blew up the Mannerheim Line, and that was that. The Germans had control of the air over Poland, Holland, Belgium, and France. In these later campaigns control of the air meant that the Germans could use the most accurate of all aerial weapons against the ground: the dive bomber. It was the Stuka dive bomber that destroyed tanks and villages, scattered troops, and disrupted communication lines. But the dive bomber can only be used in air which is first freed of defending interceptors. For it is slow, badly armed, and easy to shoot down. German propaganda to the contrary notwithstanding, no Stuka bombers are operating over England or have been for two months. The occasional references to dive bombing that have come through on the cables have referred not to true diving Stukas but to bomb-carrying pursuit ships, swooping low before releasing their bombs. Their speed and the small loads that they can carry render them ineffective.

The Germans have tried very hard to get control of the air over England, but they have not got it. They have used every kind of ship they have. They have struck from all four points of the compass, operating from convenient bases to the east and south—opposite Dover. Of course they are only a short twenty miles or approximately three minutes' flying time away.

There are two reasons why they have failed to gain control of the air over England.

The first is a machine—an electrical device which in the truest sense of the word can be said to have saved Britain. . . .

[*At the request of the British government, three paragraphs describing the technique by which enemy planes are spotted before they reach the English Coast are omitted here.*

[*This manuscript has not been submitted to the British or any other government before publication. But this chapter as originally written was checked with military authorities in this country and news of its contents were cabled to England. The Ministry of Information then wired the following request:*

[*TWO PASSAGES RELATING OUR SECRET DEVICES . . . EARNESTLY PLEAD . . . OMISSION FOR SECURITY REASONS . . . EMPHASIZE THIS VERY IMPORTANT BRITAIN.*]

The second reason why the Germans have not control of the air, as I explained before, is that the Hurricane and Spitfire, the two first-line British interceptor planes, are definitely superior as air weapons to either the Messerschmidt 109 or the twin-motor Messerschmidt 110. This superiority means that it does the Germans no good to send their Messerschmidts over above their bombers to protect them from the interceptors. The English can break up the Messerschmidts at high altitudes, shoot down the bombers below them.

So excellent is the English defense by day that it is very rare nowadays whenever one or two bombers get through the interceptors to their targets. The daylight raids you read about are not made by bombers but by pursuit ships flying at great speed and at enormous altitudes—not less than five and nearer six miles straight up in the air. As converted into bombers they are absolutely useless except when bombing such targets as the whole city of London. And then they can only peck away.

As to the effectiveness of this kind of bombing I give you this example: I have stood on an airport on the edge of London. Before the war it was a commercial airport and German pilots flew planes in and out of it. They must know it as they know the palm of their own hand. I was shown a map which recorded every single bomb that was dropped on the field since the *blitz* began. I counted fifty-six hits. This field had been hit fifty-six separate times and yet had never been out of operation for an hour. The total damage was:

An empty hangar destroyed by concussion from a land mine.

A training plane annihilated.

A visiting Spitfire which was parked on a runway destroyed.

And this field, to repeat, is one of the best known in England and has been in continuous use as an RAF military airport since the war began!

The only kind of bombing the Germans can still do is that kind of bombing which can be done without control of the air. To wit: bombing at night. In regard to bombing by night these facts are pertinent: antiaircraft is ineffective in defense, hits very few planes because of the difficulty of aiming at an unseen plane in the dark. But the antiaircraft is credited with keeping enemy planes at high altitudes—at least of over four miles. At lower altitudes their fire becomes more accurate and they are apt to be picked up by the searchlights on the ground, whose lights reach about four miles.

At four or five miles above the ground over a black-out country, accuracy in bombing is extremely difficult.

It is made much easier by moonlight. The moonlight

reflects on surface water—lakes, ponds, rivers—and guides the bombing pilots. That is why unless some way is found to intercept night bombers damage from night raiding will always be much greater when the moon is full. All you have to do to predict damaging night raids over London in advance is to consult your almanac (or damaging night raids over Germany).

The most exciting and momentous research now in progress in England—and probably in Germany, too—is research into methods of intercepting night bombers. When as and if a holeproof method is found, death and destruction in the dark will be defeated and the whole Hitlerian technique based on terror will have to be revised—because bombing by night is the last card in his hand which can still take tricks.

As to where this research stands, the English have a device with which . . .

[*At the request of the British government a second deletion is made here.*]

And *coup de grâce* it is because night fighters do not really fight. They simply strike down in the dark.

The night fighter's problem is not how to kill, which is easy once it has located its enemy, but how to locate it. The enemy it seeks to destroy is moving through the air at 300 or more miles an hour somewhere between three and six miles high. Without eyes, with eyes only of electricity, it must locate its enemy and bring itself close enough so that the pilot can see when and where to strike. The practical distance for night killing is 100 yards and that is very close to get to an unseen pin point in infinity.

The pilots who fight by night are chosen after exhaustive tests. It has been found true that one man sees better than another in the dark. There are men whose eyes are more nearly like the eyes of a cat. When these men fight at night their night vision is found to improve by the administration of drugs which affect the nerves and muscles of the eye and improve their sight in the dark. That is why they are able to shoot straight at 100 yards while moving several hundred miles an hour in the black.

When as and if this device is really perfected so that it can be used not merely experimentally but practically night after night and on a large scale, the night bomber will be finished. Because it has no defense whatever against a night fighter's cannon crashing into it out of nothing. The attack is always a surprise attack. It is all over before the crew in the bomber know what has happened to them.

But for the practical purposes of maintaining industrial production and defending military objectives, the RAF has already won by confining German mass bombing to night raids.

As to particulars of night-bombing accuracy it is now well established that many of the bombs dropped by the Germans on London are not released by the bomber in the plane but are dropped automatically by radio control from the German base. Air-minded Americans are already familiar with the radio beam by which our commercial ships fly out of sight of land through fog from one port to another. The German night bombers come over Britain on radio beams from occupied France. These beams are crossed over London with beams coming from German-occupied Norway. The pilot simply steers his course along the beam from the south. When his ship intersects the beam from the east his bomb load is released automatically.

The flaw in this ingenious arrangement is . . .

[*At the request of the British government a third deletion is made here.*]

Hence the phenomenon I have already noted on the ground, of the German bombs all around but rarely on their objective.

The automatic release is of course not the only device the Germans use. As I have said, they also bomb by moonlight on the ground water—and the English are already moving to check this by coating ground water with a black film wherever possible—and when they are able to light a fire they bomb by its light. Flares don't seem so effective. I have seen them drop and those I saw seemed to go out too high in the sky to light the ground. Others I am told are shot down by machine gunning the parachutes as they descend. You must also realize that these night bombers *can* sometimes be reached by anti-aircraft fire. They are not invulnerable. The big six-inch guns in London—some of them moved in the week I was there—can explode their shell seven miles up in the air. The shell fragments are fatal to airplanes within fifty yards surrounding the explosion, if they are not given protection. They get some hits.

In discussing the famed American bomb sight as a case in point it was said to me by a bombing pilot that he doubted its definitive effect on the course of the war because he didn't care how accurate it might be in the dry, calm air over Texas. He didn't think any bomb sight conceivable could solve his problem of how to lower his bomb on his target at night through clouds with anti-aircraft bursting all around him. And if he got near so that he could really see his target, the bomb sight he had was plenty good enough.

I have described German operations over England in this much detail to give you some picture of what I mean when I say that the RAF fighter command has licked Hermann Goering's *Luftwaffe* and that having licked it German bomb operations you read about in the paper every day are without important military significance. If

— 177 —

the Germans were able to break the morale of the people by night bombing, that would be something else again. But as long as the British fighter command continues to get the better of the *Luftwaffe* fighting arm, that is an end to the kind of terror from the air that broke the Mannerheim Line, that annihilated Poland, that swept Holland, Belgium, and France before it. That is why the English countryside is so peaceful, why the factory chimneys smoke, why people cross rivers on bridges and trains run, and why the most characteristic sight of London is still civilians peacefully going about their business, hardly stopping to look up during a daylight raid.

The most universal answer in England to my question, "How do you propose to win the war" was "by mass bombing of German industrial plants with planes built in America—mass bombing from the air behind a blockade by sea."

The reasoning behind these statements is something like this:

If the British are able to exchange bomb for bomb with the Germans, the blockade will decide the war. For when German industrial capacity is destroyed it cannot be replaced—whereas when British industrial capacity is destroyed the British, with the sea lanes open, can draw on American industrial capacity. This, of course, is an oversimplification, but it conveys the idea.

I am often asked about the British bombing of Germany. Is it effective? I have seen so much ineffective bombing by the Germans in England that I am very skeptical about any claims to industrial damage wrought by bombs. The Germans have done little damage to England's industrial plant because it is so well dispersed, broken up into small units with no one plant indispensable. I have no reason to believe that the Germans aren't just as good at this business of dispersal of industrial equipment.

There is only this reason to believe that the English bombing of the German industrial plant may be less effective than its opposite number: the English, possibly because they have fewer planes, do not bomb as many objectives or over as wide an area as the Germans. The British theory of bombing is that it should be concentrated on the fewest possible number of key objectives and that it should be practically continuous. That is, they pick out a plant and bomb it every single night that they can get to it, week in and week out. Whereas the Germans—it is easily observable from the communiqués—follow the practice of concentrating on one place one night, another place another night—and mix the bombing of industrial objectives with scatter bombing for the sole purpose of attacking civilian morale by the destruction of civilian property and the killing of noncombatants. Thus, considering every thousand bombs dropped by the Germans as against every thousand bombs dropped by the English, it is possible that a higher percentage of the English bombs do damage to industrial production than vice versa.

The English bombing of Berlin—this is my own conclusion—is a propaganda rather than a military operation. I was not convinced that the RAF bomber command thought it was doing much damage to Berlin or expected to do much damage to Berlin. The idea is simply to keep the Germans in Berlin running in and out of shelters.

The RAF bombing is concentrated on the Ruhr and military objects along the coast.

On its present scale, the English bombing of Germany must be no more than a very unpleasant nuisance to the Germans. It will not become more than this until the English fleet of bombers is enormously increased. And this increased fleet will have to be manned by the pilots now training in Canada and Australia. The first are just finishing their courses, but the new bombing pilots will not be available in large numbers until late in the spring. Bomber crews must be carefully selected, are highly specialized, and take a long time to train. A first-class pilot should have at least nine months' schooling and practice.

The British are not relying solely on our bombing planes to achieve superiority, but have new models of their own in production. They are bigger than any airplanes I have ever seen, including transatlantic clippers, and when you stand below and look up at them and their bomb bay is open, it's as if the biggest whale you can conceive of were hoisted to the top of Madison Square Garden and its belly slit from nose to tail.

The British are entirely confident that with their own production, American production, and pilots from the Empire they will be ready to go into Germany en masse by spring. Not the least important feature of their present bombing operations over Germany is the training of crews. Crews are rotated, a bombing pilot being only used on active raiding over enemy territory for a month —after which he stops fighting and goes back to school— either to instruct or to learn another of the varied trades included in a bomber's crew. He must not merely be an expert heavy-plane pilot, but also an expert in machine gunnery and in wireless and in navigation.

Next to the Fire Department in London, the RAF as a whole is the best show I saw in England. Its long-term planning and its efficiency are very convincing. My confidence that England can and will win is based in important part on my confidence that the RAF can and will carry out its program.

Beyond the mass bombing of the German industrial plant lies the further dream: the dream that with American production behind it and the whole Empire producing pilots, the RAF can move across the Channel to defeat the *Luftwaffe* on its own ground and gain real control of the air. When and as that day comes the show will be over—

for, to go back to what I said a long time ago in this book
—ineffective and haphazard as night bombing is, with
real control of the air by day the nation on the offensive
is practically irresistible and can do what it likes—smash
up a Mannerheim Line as the Russians did in Finland,
destroy the communications of an army as the Germans
did in Poland, or destroy whatever plant it cares to as
the Germans did again in Holland. With control of German air the British could polish Hitler off in short order.

Along the road between the present scale of offensive
bombing and the total annihilation of the German Air
Force, the politicians of England—as distinct from the
military men in the Air Force who are solely interested
in military superiority—the politicians believe that the
German morale will crack. They believe that there will
come a point at which the Germans cannot take it. The
process of suggesting to the Germans that this is what's
going to happen has already begun. The English bombers over Germany carry not only bombs but propaganda
leaflets. The tone of these propaganda leaflets is quite
different from that of the leaflets which used to be flown
over the Maginot Line and which tended to suggest that
all men were brothers and what's all the shooting about.
The leaflets that the RAF is scattering with their bombs
are aggressive and belligerent. Their theme is bomb for
bomb, terror for terror. The leaflet that is reproduced on
page 185 flew in a British bombing plane over Berlin.
Why the pilot did not drop it, how it came about that
this leaflet returned to England, is a story worth telling.

After flying x miles to drop it on Berlin, the ship came in
hot just before dawn. All the rest of the squadron had got
back an hour earlier. They'd reported that none of them
had reached Berlin. High over the German countryside
they had met a snowstorm, seen that they couldn't get
through it, and turned about to bomb their secondary objectives on their way home. The crew of the plane that

came in hot reported that they had reached the edge of Berlin. They added that they had lost their aerial there—their trailing aerial, the long wire that they unwind behind their plane while they are in flight. It had caught on some object on the ground and been torn off.

While they were having breakfast the story came out.

The bomber they flew was an Armstrong-Whitley. Its complement is a crew of six. There are the gunner who sits in the tail and the gunner in the nose turret. There's the bomber who lies on his belly underneath the pilots' feet. There are the two pilots who sit side by side as in a transport plane, and the radio operator whose desk and apparatus are just behind them. There's a catwalk down the middle of the bomber which leads out to the rear gunner in the tail. It's a narrow wooden catwalk and along its sides cables are strung so that a man walking up it may hang on when the air is rough. He can almost but not quite stand up. Leaving his turret and coming forward he passes the wires that lead to the tail controls—the flippers and the rudder. He passes the little toilet seat, walking above the bomb racks. And up abreast of the wings he reaches the place where the radio operator sits, and below and in front of him are the pilots. This is convenient because if he's wounded one of the pilots, who is also a gunner, can get back down the catwalk and take his place.

It was clear over England when this bomber took off and it met no bad weather until it reached the German-held coast. It was flying at 15,000 feet then and still climbing. The weather got very bad in a great hurry. It was extremely rough in the plane, but the pilot went on on instruments and climbed to 20,000 feet. A hundred miles from Berlin the ship began to feel heavy on the controls and he knew he was taking on more ice than he should. The plane would no longer climb. But he was close to his objective and he thought he might as well go on through.

The pilot didn't remember exactly how it happened, but the ship began to fall off on one wing and no matter what he did he couldn't bring up the dropped wing and then all of a sudden the plane went smack over onto its back and into a spin. With a full bomb load still in its belly. And it was right in a cloudful of snow and ice. The plane wound up—that is, spinning, its spin became tighter and tighter until it whipped around on its own axis like a top.

The spin started at 20,000 feet. When the ship passed 10,000 feet the rear gunner broke. He climbed down out of his glass eggshell and lowered himself along the catwalk, which was now standing on end and revolving rapidly. His parachute on his tail and his Mae West on his chest, he wrestled his way along the guy ropes on either side of the catwalk until his head came abreast of the wireless operator's.

He said to the wireless operator: "I've had enough. I'm going out."

He was a big man and he filled all the space there was between the wireles operator and the other side of the plane. The wireless operator was a little man and a cockney. He didn't know what was going to happen to the ship and he didn't know how to handle the situation. All he could think of to say was: "What for?"

There was some kind of argument between the radio operator and the rear gunner that neither of them could remember very well, except that the radio operator arrived at the observation that they must be too low to make jumping worth while, anyway.

The plane still was whipping violently around its self-appointed axis. A few seconds below 10,000 feet the pilot told the bomber to let go everything. The bombs went—on nonmilitary objectives.

No one could remember how it stopped, either. The pilot was kicking at his rudder and trying to reverse the controls, but for four miles coming down he'd been doing that and nothing had happened before. Then all of a sudden there was a tremor that ran through the ship like an electric shock and all of a sudden it stopped spinning and there it was, right side up, flying it didn't know where, or how far above the ground. It was not until the crew got back to England that they found the trailing aerial‾missing and knew that that's what had caused the tremor, its getting torn off on some object on the ground. The radio operator said he was pretty sure they'd torn it off on the flagpole on the Reichstag—but only pretty sure because, he added reflectively, he was still arguing with the rear gunner about whether there was enough altitude left to make jumping worth while.

As they told the story at breakfast, the pilot who hadn't said much suddenly snapped his fingers.

"Good Lord," he said, "I forgot the leaflets."

The man he was having breakfast with said: "What leaflets?"

He said: "The leaflets I was supposed to drop with the bombs. I just forgot all about them."

He called for an orderly and sent him out to where the plane was parked. It was getting light. The orderly brought back the bundle of leaflets and the pilot took one off the top and said to his visitor:

"Would you like one for a souvenir?"

The bomber said:

"I wonder where those bombs hit."

The radio operator answered that he couldn't be certain, of course, but he was pretty sure that they demolished a maternity hospital.

The rear gunner said:

"I was through, you know. I wanted to jump."

Everybody laughed.

TERROR !

TERROR war Hitlers Waffe als er das deutsche Volk und Reich seiner Partei dienstbar machte.

TERROR war Hitlers Waffe gegen Österreich, die Tschechoslowakei, Polen, Norwegen, Terror gegen Wehrlose, Mord an Waffenlosen, Brandstiftung an unverteidigten Städten.

TERROR hemmungsloser, vorbedachter Terror zwang Holland, Belgien und das uneinige Frankreich auf die Kniee.

TERROR sollte auch Englands Kampfeswillen brechen. Aber

Ihr habt Euch verrechnet!

Gegen die sprichwörtliche Gleichmütigkeit, gegen die eisernen Nerven, gegen den sturen Willen der Briten vermögen Görings Bomben nichts. Tag für Tag wird Euch diese Lehre deutlicher beigebracht.

BOMBEN WIDER BOMBEN !

Das ist unsere Antwort an Hitler: Bomben und immer mehr Bomben.

BOMBEN auf die Kasernen, auf die Kriegshäfen, auf die Flugplätze.

BOMBEN auf die Kruppwerke, auf Spandau, auf Augsburg, auf Magdeburg.

BOMBEN auf alle Benzinfabriken, auf Leuna, Misburg, Pöhlitz.

BOMBEN auf die deutsche Kriegsmaschine. Bomben immer tiefer nach Osten hinein.

WIR SCHLAGEN ZURÜCK !

BOMBEN ÜBER DEUTSCHLAND — bis 5. Oktober

In den auf dieser Karte dargestellten Städten wurden militärische Objekte durch die britische Luftwaffe bombardiert. Die Bombenangriffe werden immer umfangreicher.

Das nachstehende Städteverzeichnis ist nur eine Auslese. Die Ziffern bedeuten die Zahl der auf die einzelnen Städte bis 5. Oktober stattgefundenen Bombenangriffe.

ZEICHENERKLÄRUNG

(fett, die zerstörten oder beschädigten militärischen Ziele):

F — Flugplätze, Flughäfen für Seeflugzeuge, Flugzeugfabriken, Flugzeuglager

S — Kriegshäfen, Stützpunkte der Kriegsmarine, Docks, Landungsplätze, Häfen, Hafendämme, Kanäle, Schiffswerfte, Boote

T — Öl-, Petroleum- und Benzinlager, Raffinerien, Tanks, Fabrikanlagen der Treibstoffproduktion

B — Bahnlinien, Knotenpunkte, Rangier- und Güterbahnhof, Verladungsplätze

W — Munitionsbetriebe, Hochöfen, chemische Werke, Kraft-(Elektrizitäts) werke

M — Munitionslager

Unter den zerstörten oder schwer beschädigten kriegswichtigen Betrieben befinden sich:

Bayer Sprengstoffwerke (Leverkusen), Bayrische Motorenwerke (München), Blohm u. Voss-Werft (Hamburg), Bosch Akkumulatoren (Stuttgart), Daimler-Benz (Stuttgart), Deutsche Schiff- u. Maschinenbau (Bremen), Dornier (Wenzendorf und Wismar), Finyler (Kassel), I. G. Farben (Leuna), Junkers (Bernburg und Dessau), Krupp (Essen), Messerschmitt (Gotha und Augsburg), Mockau-Erla (Leipzig), Rheinische Kraftwerke (Köln), Siemens u. Schuckert (Berlin), Zeiss (Jena).

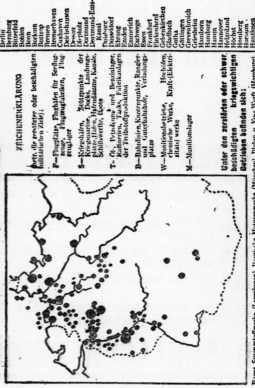

Ort	Ziel	Bomben-angriffe	Ort	Ziel	Bomben-angriffe
Aachen	F B	3	Kast.-op-Rauxel	T	3
Augsburg	F B	3	Kettersloch	W	1
Berlin	F T B W	17	Kiel	S T	18
Bernburg	W	2	Korbrn	W	1
Bitterfeld	F	2	Köln	F T B W	33
Bohlen	T	1	Krefeld	F B M	13
Bonn	F B	4	Kölleda	F	3
Borkum	T	1	Leipzig	W	3
Bottrop	F B	10	Leuna	T	2
Bremen	F S T B	6	Leverkusen	W	4
Bremerhaven	S	3	Lippstadt	B W	9
Cuxhaven	S	1	Lingen	T B W	6
Deichhausen	P	1	Ludwigshafen	T B W	11
Dessau	F T	5	Lünen	B W	17
Dörpholz	F	1	Magdeburg	F T B W	11
Dortmund	F T B W M	14	Mannheim	T B	4
Dortmund-Ems-Kanal			Monheim	T W	7
Duisburg	S T W	11	Misburg	P	2
Ehrang	B T M	7	Münster	F B	14
Emden	S T B	9	Neckarium	T	22
Emmerich	B	1	Nordrney	P S	5
Eschwege	B W	5	Osnabrück	B M	3
Essen	T W	17	Osterfeld	B M	6
Finkenherd	T	12	Paderborn	F M	1
Frankfurt	B T W		Politz	T	2
Gelsenkirchen	B W	20	Quakenbrück	P	5
Gladbach	B W	3	Regensburg	F	4
Gotha	F	2	Reisholz	T W	2
Göttingen	F T	3	Rheinberg	B	3
Grevenbroich	W	2	Recklinghausen	B M	10
Griesheim	F	1	Rhcine	B	30
Hamborn	S T B W	37	Ruhrort-Hafen	B	4
Hamburg	B M B	63	Salzbergen	B M	1
Hanau	F T B		Schwerte	B M	13
Hannover	S M	20	Soest	T W	5
Heligoland	S W	8	Sterkrade	W	22
Höchst	T B	3	Stuttgart	T B	6
Homberg	W	12	Wanne-Eickel	F	1
Horsum	F	1	Warnemünde	F T B W	5
Huntlosen	F	2	Wesel	S T	22
Jena	T B	1	Wenzendorf	F S	8
Kamen	W	6	Wilhelmshaven		
Kassel	F W	6	Wismar		

XIII

THE HARDEST QUESTIONS

THE HARDEST questions to answer about the English are how they are going to win the war and what they are going to do when they've won it. The general belief in the government as well as in the Air Force is that it can and will be won by intensive bombing of Germany. It is recognized that this can be done only with American production of bombing planes and after the Empire pilot-training program is at least six months, possibly a year, older. The theory is that the industrial production of Germany can be crippled until Hitler hollers for help. The Greek show and the Middle East show are regarded as important but not crucial. But I don't think many people I have talked to would call me a liar if I said flatly that the heads of the British government do not know how the war is to be won. They simply propose to find out how and to win it. There was a great deal of talk about taking the offensive while I was there— somewhere in the Mediterranean, even in the north. But most of it was a bombing offensive on German industrial production.

As to the postwar world—the most intelligent people seem to be increasingly conscious of their obligation to define their objectives. But they are yet to be defined.

The government, I believe, is thinking in terms of some kind of United States of Europe, disarmed, on the ground, and policed by an international air force—and the world then to take up where it left off in its search for social justice.

I went to England full of such questions as these. It did not take me long to find out how deeply uninterested people who are fighting for life as they know it—and fighting desperately with their backs to the wall—are in that long view of history on which peaceful peoples like to speculate.

That fundamental changes are taking place in Great Britain there is no doubt. But as to estimating how far they have progressed, or appraising their permanence— that is a subject that is interesting to speculate on but not very profitable. A cynic remarked to me that the most terrible thing that could happen to England was to have the Germans stop bombing it. There may be some truth in this statement. As long as the bombs do not kill too many people, and yet are still falling, England will continue to change, and for what we in America will think the better. Class snobbery, so offensive to us whether in lords and ladies or truck drivers or scullery maids, is forcibly breaking down. A nation cannot sleep wherever it finds itself at night and with whomever happens to lie down next to it and not have things happen to its class distinctions. A nation cannot be in such desperate need of skill and so deeply indebted to whoever has it regardless of class without things happening to it. A nation cannot go bankrupt cheerfully as England is going bankrupt within the next six months without things happening to social relations based on capital and property. But as to how far this process has gone, and whether when the war is over the scullery maids and the ladies in waiting will go back to their old relationships, I would not venture to say.

What I do know is that, whatever its cost, "the war effort" is a really universal effort—a tide in which every man, woman, and child swims; and that there are few back eddies and waters in which this is not so. It was this universality of effort that I met everywhere that made the government seem to me somehow, and curiously, unimportant. It is as if it were not guiding events, but being pushed by them. Not simply by external events, but by things happening internally in England. The government is not even as possessive about the war as the Communist Party is possessive about the shelters. And in almost every single minister of the government I talked to I felt a sense of men being pushed from below, of trying to keep up with the demands of the people— whether their problems are fighting the Germans in the air, maintaining the position of labor and production, or of protecting people on the ground from war in the air.

In direct answer to the questions, "Do you believe there is a social revolution in England? And if so, in what direction?" I would have no hesitancy answering.

"Yes. To the Left."

APPENDIX

I find there still remain many odds and ends of information in my head. I am jotting them down below as they come, without concern for relative importance or order. Some of them you will find newsworthy. Others are purely anecdotal.

DAMAGE TO INDUSTRIAL PRODUCTION

Just before I got to London, *PM*'s Ben Robertson returned from a trip through the Midlands and Scotland. I did not try to duplicate his rounds. The industrial establishments I visited were around London and southern England. I talked with other American correspondents who had been other places, with English journalists and with friends and connections—and finally with Lord Beaverbrook, who is in charge of aircraft production and whom I knew casually from a visit to England some years before. Putting all this evidence into one generality:

A number of industrial establishments producing military aircraft or parts therefor were severely damaged during the first two weeks in September. Other industrial properties, military and nonmilitary, were also damaged at this time. Since the last of the successful mass daylight raids on September 15, German bombers have done very little damage to industrial plants. The damage done in the early part of September has been repaired, so that there is agreement that military production in England is again at or within a few per cent of production at the beginning of September.

It is hard to say whether this is good news or bad. Great Britain had been increasing its production steadily until the first of September. But for the bomb damage then its production would be much higher now. But on the other hand, the September damage has been repaired and production is now increasing steadily.

I found no evidence that any material news of industrial damage was currently being suppressed—although there is no doubt that in September the British did minimize the effects of a very severe blow dealt to them then.

One device by which the British are currently maintaining and increasing production is by the training and stationing of spotters on the roofs of factories engaged in twenty-four-hour- production. With a trained spotter on the roof—a spotter who can distinguish his own from enemy aircraft and who is familiar with the ways of bombs and bombers—workers in the factory may continue at their posts until the last minute when safety demands they leave their work and go to the shelters. Good spotters have improved the morale in factories.

Industrial production is dispersed well. No single factory's total destruction could stop the production of a vital part of the war machine.

While many people criticize the effectiveness of the balloon barrage over London, there has never been a successful dive-bombing operation against a factory protected by a tight balloon barrage.

This factory makes airplane motors and is guarded by local squadrons. One afternoon in September a large flight of enemy bombers was reported approaching it. The fighters took to the air. The bombers arrived, passed the factory, and were chased across country by the fighters. As soon as the fighters were out of sight, a second German squadron appeared and let go on the factory. Damage would have been greater had not the bomber squadron been attacked by a lone English fighter, who dove into it with such abandon that he partially broke the formation. Eyewitnesses described this to me. But the factory was hit and was out of production for some weeks.

THE BOMBING HISTORY OF ONE FACTORY

The second half of the story:

A short time after this same factory was in production again, the Germans played the same trick. The fighter squadrons again went after the first flight. There was a low ceiling of clouds four or five thousand feet up. The second flight of bombers came on schedule just under the clouds. But as they approached the plant the defending pursuit ships came down out of the clouds in a solid formation. They had pretended to be lured into the trap and now took their vengeance. The bombers were cut to bits, never reached their target. The factory is in full production and has not been hit since.

NO SHORTAGE OF FIGHTERS

I gathered much evidence around various airports, including experimental ones, confirming the fact that there was no shortage of Spitfires or Hurricanes in England. There are enough, for instance, so that many squadrons are being re-equipped with equipment that increases the range and maximum altitude at which they can fight. And new squadrons of newly trained men are going into action. (There was similar evidence that there is no shortage of pilot material. The only complaint I heard was from fighter pilots who felt they were being forced to take too much rest.)

THE BAD NEWS

The bad news in Great Britain while I was there was not of the air war, which was daily perfecting its defensive and offensive technique, but of the less publicized submarine war. It was generally known amongst the informed that losses from submarine action were "too high," "serious." This was before losses from the German raider were reported.

Mr. Cross, who is the Minister for Shipping, told me that what he thought Great Britain needed from America was not planes but small, fast cargo ships. Small so that there could be a lot of them. Fast so that they could get away from submarines. The submarine is very successful in stalking a convoy moving at twelve knots or less. It can locate its prey without coming up, maneuvering underwater to within striking distance. Within striking distance a big convoy is easy prey for a submarine. All it has to do is to loose all its torpedoes one after another in a straight line across the convoy's path. Some of the torpedoes are bound to hit some of the ships.

Many informed people in Great Britain suspect that the submarines are using bases in Ireland. There are many stories of submarine crews being seen in the cafés in Dublin out of uniform. Whether German submarines do or do not use Ireland, they have nevertheless reversed the disadvantage they were under in the last war. This was:

In the last war German submarines entered the Atlantic through the narrow Channel. The British surrounded this opening and the British in turn had a wide base for their own shipping across the Atlantic, being able to sail to and from any port in the British Isles. Now this position is exactly reversed. British shipping must enter the Atlantic from a narrow base—the ports on the west coast of England. Whereas the Germans—leaving Ireland out of it—can operate their submarines from widely separated bases, all the German-held coast being available. The English still try to mine up the German submarines, of course, and the English shipping can hardly be said to be bottled up as the Germans were in the last war. But broadly speaking the tables *are turned* and the small German submarine fleet is making the most of it.

Members of the Air Force thought that when they were richer in American reconnoissance planes they could cut down these submarine losses by wider and wider patrols.

But as of this writing I consider submarine warfare the most successful and dangerous of all the Fascists' various operations against Great Britain.

ON THE SUBJECT OF IRELAND

Ben Robertson has recently noted in *PM* that at night the city of Dublin shows the only lights between New York and Moscow. It also shows the only lights between Lisbon and Sweden. It is lit so brightly that every night the German bombers come over and circle and check their bearings. The RAF is as mad about Dublin's being a beacon to the enemy aviators as you would expect.

HOW MUCH WORK IT IS TO BE BOMBED

One cannot move around London more than a few days without being impressed by how busy a city is that is being bombed. People have written about how terrible bombs are, or how inconvenient or how exciting it is to be bombed. Nobody has written about how much work it is; but that is the most striking thing of all. It is twenty-four-hours-a-day work for millions of people. Every morning the ruins of the night before must be cleaned up. Telephone and gas lines and water mains repaired. The business of bringing food and supplies into the city carries its load of inconvenience and added labor. The smallest white-collar clerk may have added work to do at home repairing his own house, helping his neighbors, chipping in his spare time as one of scores of volunteers. And the act of getting to and from his office may be more work to him. The work of putting out fires is multiplied ten- or twentyfold. The sheer work of keeping a city in operation while it is being bombed is appalling.

THE WOMEN IN LONDON

If I remember correctly there are 8000 women workers called the WVS—the Women's Volunteer Service. They are equipped in an unbecoming, dark-blue uniform—all the women's uniforms in England seem to me unbecoming. These women volunteers do everything from driving ambulances to running canteens which drive from bombing to bombing bringing warm drinks and food to the ARP workers there.

I watched only one unit in operation. I wasn't impressed with its efficiency. It was morning, and five or six women were loading up a trailer to go to the scene of the last night's bombings. They had to stock it with tea and sandwiches and I presume certain items of cutlery and china. I watched them for an hour. They were still running back and forth to the cellar for things they had forgotten. They reminded me of the housewives of a small village preparing a light refreshment for a charity bazaar. I gathered from remarks under the breath that the two slaveys who were helping them in the canteen felt the same way. One of the latter said out of the side of her mouth to me: "I have never been out of work before nor worked so hard," and went back to polishing a counter that didn't need to be polished.

It would undoubtedly do the ladies a severe injustice to generalize from this specific instance.

But I like the WAAF's much better. WAAF means Women's Air Auxiliary Force. A Waaf is a young lady in active military service. Collectively she is the secretariat of the Air Force. All the Air Force officers I talked to about the Waafs were very enthusiastic about them—said they were hard-working, efficient, professional. One said to me thoughtfully, "There's really much less immorality than you'd think, you know."

I liked the air-raid warden whom I met playing chess with the old man in the shelter she looked after. She wore blue dungarees and a steel helmet painted blue and looked very attractive in them. She wasn't as professional as the Waafs I met but she made sense talking about her job.

Coming in and out of the Dorchester by day you still see ladies in mink coats and high heels, wearing flowers. The nails are very well polished and the hair excellently waved.

In waiting for busses around dusk I would guess that one out of every ten women I saw wore trousers. They appeared to be women who worked in shops or offices. They were not self-conscious about wearing trousers and they looked better than I expected they would. The trousers were neither floppy nor fancy. They appeared to be cut in straight lines. As Miss Hawes in *PM* has suggested they should, most of them wore coats about as long as a man's coat—or longer.

The ladies officers took out to dance wore evening dresses and were very pretty.

The women who slept in shelters wore no special costumes. But I saw a number of the younger ones in shelters improvising beauty treatments for themselves—doing their hair in front of propped-up mirrors, working on their faces.

I did not see many women taking tickets in busses or sharing other usually male jobs as they did in the last war—except in the WAAF, as already noted.

A number of people spoke to me at length about how well women behaved during bombings. They said they were not as emotionally disturbed as one might expect, that they took things gamely and kept their heads. The ones I talked to certainly behaved with remarkable fortitude about the loss of their homes and the disruption of their lives by the war.

THE SHOPS OF LONDON

Are all open and you can buy anything you like. Only the food is rationed as I have described. Even the stores that are bombed out are open. A sign reading BUSINESS AS USUAL is a common sight tacked across the face of some ruins. Sometimes the sign reads, BUSINESS AS USUAL—IN OUR NEW STORE ON THE NEXT STREET. One of the big department stores—not one of the biggest, but a big one—was bombed out in September. I visited a couple of others and found them intact, although one had sustained several minor bomb injuries.

THE POLES IN ENGLAND

There are 1800 Polish pilots in England and four or five thousand other Polish soldiers. The Polish pilots are the talk of London. They are all veterans and they are the most experienced fighter pilots in the British Air Force. Almost every squadron has a Pole or two attached to it and the Poles also have a squadron of their own. There was a funny story on the censorship around London when I was there. The censorship refused to pass the true statement that the Polish squadron had the finest record in the RAF for destroying German planes. English commanders in the RAF were outraged. They were back of the Poles and they wanted them to get credit for their record. So they appealed to the censorship. After some debate the following statement was passed: "The Polish command of the Polish Squadron *says* its record is the best in the RAF."

The Poles wear regular RAF uniforms with little labels on the arms just below the shoulders: Poland. Few of them speak any English. At the beginning of the war they were very nervous about the possibility of having to bail out over England and come down in their parachutes. They were afraid that because they did not speak English people would shoot them for Germans. So every Pole was taught to parrot these sentences: "I am a Pole. I am a member of the Royal Air Force. I am a Pole. I am a member of the Royal Air Force."

People say now that when Poles who are shot down reappear at headquarters they always have a girl on each arm. They say the girls cannot resist the Poles, nor the Poles the girls.

Their squadron is in Scotland. They say that instead of the Poles learning English the storekeepers are learning Polish. The Polish names, of course, are unpronounceable, and when Poles are attached to English squadrons they usually get nicknames. One I met was called Lieutenant Whisky.

When talking to one Pole I led with my chin and asked: "Why are you fighting in England?" He said very simply: "Because my mother, who is sixty-five years old, is carrying coal for a living in Warsaw." I changed the subject.

England is full of dreadful tales of what the German government is doing in Poland. It is also full of very interesting tales about things that individual German soldiers and officers have done. Many letters are smuggled out of Poland by German officers traveling via Vichy and Lisbon. Some German officers do not carry out the more barbaric orders. Others lend food and money to those they are there to persecute. Everyone feels that the Germans have singled out the Poles as a people to be—literally—destroyed. The able-bodied men are taken from Poland to Germany. The women are worked or starved or both. Young male children between twelve and eighteen are castrated.

There is no indication that the Polish aviators in England disbelieve these stories. They fight in the air with great abandon and courage.

EVE CURIE

Not the least interesting person in London, daughter of the great scientist. Her mother, Mme Curie, was a Pole, and she works for the restoration of Poland as well as for a free France. She is handsome, chic, and intelligent and has great knowledge of European politics. She knew most members of the French government well and her criticism of them was so outspoken that she barely escaped from France. She lives in the Dorchester Hotel. Does not sleep in a shelter. Is writing a series of lectures to be given when she comes here in January.

I talked with her about the chances of a revolution in France against the Germans and the Vichy government. I gathered she did not think the chances were very good now and that people were still too confused. I asked her

about Dakar, saying that I felt very strongly that even if
De Gaulle had misjudged his reception there the British
fleet should have taken the place anyway. She did not
defend De Gaulle but said she doubted if Americans
realized—if anyone but a Frenchman could realize—what
a terrible impression the sinking of the French fleet at
Oran had had on the French people. She thought it had
alienated them from the British more than any other
one thing, and that it was because of this effect of the
sinking at Oran that the British had not wanted to risk
another bad reaction by using British guns at Dakar. But
still she thought Dakar was very unfortunate.

She said she felt that Britain was the only hope for
France and for the world and for that reason she was
doing and would do everything she could for the British.
She is very popular in London. Everyone likes her.

THE CIVIL SERVICE

Most people feel that the Civil Service of which the
British were once so proud has completely fallen down
in the present crisis. Too hide-bound to stand the pressure of war work—all brains and no sense. A member of
the Cabinet described it to me as: "A device to exercise
authority without accepting responsibility," and added
that as such it was a liability in wartime.

BUSINESS AS USUAL

The hardest thing in the world to get into anybody's
head is the commonplace. I have told friends a hundred
times—and I have written and printed it in my newspaper
—that neither bombs nor bomb damage nor even 8000
people sleeping in rows in a subway are the really typical,
characteristic sights of London. A really typical, really
characteristic sight is the sight of people going peacefully

about their business by day, paying no attention whatever to the demolished buildings they pass every block or two or the puffs of antiaircraft shells that may be breaking over their heads. The most striking and dramatic fact about London is none of these things, but—just because we in America are educated by headlines, and therefore do not expect it—the most striking and dramatic fact is "business as usual."

"Business as usual" means just what it implies. It means people getting up and going to work by bus to the same offices at the same salaries. It means people buying food and cooking and eating it. It means women worrying about their hair and men fussing over shaving mirrors. In a nation of shopkeepers it means keeping shop. In a nation of trade unionists it means paying dues to the union and attending meetings and organizing shop committees. It means being a little late and forgetting a telephone number and worrying about it. It means getting drunk on Saturday night.

Business as usual in London means just what it says. By day. Not by night, but by day. The night is something else again. But by day it's business as usual. It really is. How can I make it clear? There is a sense of frustration about trying to convey something so commonplace. I know no better way than to reprint a letter—a business communication on the well-known letterhead of Selfridge & Co., Ltd. Those who care to may call it a masterpiece of British understatement, of faultless commercial calm. Whatever it is, it's one of the few exhibits I have from London about which I can honestly and genuinely and without qualification say the word "Typical." The letter:

DEAR MADAM:

As you have doubtless read in the Press, on the night of the 18th inst. we were selected by enemy raiders as a "Military Objective," but fortunately the Store only received slight damage and had it not been for the delayed action bombs in the neighborhood we should have opened as usual the following morning.

The fact that the authorities prevented us from opening caused a certain amount of inconvenience to our customers, which is much regretted, although in co-operation with our associate House, William Whiteley, we endeavoured to fulfill all Provision orders and to deliver on time all rationed food stuffs.

If by any chance you were put to any inconvenience, we feel sure you will appreciate that the circumstances were entirely beyond our control, but we are happy to inform you that every department in the Store (including the Provision Section) is now functioning quite normally.

With compliments,
Yours faithfully,
SELFRIDGE & CO., LTD.

ABOUT THE AUTHOR

Before Ralph Ingersoll launched New York's new five-cent tabloid, PM, *of which he is also the editor, he had three careers behind him. He took his Bachelor of Science degree from Yale in 1921 and spent the next two years as a miner and a mining engineer in California, Arizona, and Mexico. He then put in two years as a reporter on the* New York American, *but in 1925 he shifted to magazine work. He served as managing editor of* The New Yorker *for five years, and in 1930 went over to* Fortune *as managing editor. In 1935 he became vice-president and general manager of Time, Inc., and two years later was appointed publisher of the magazine,* Time. *Soon after, however, he left* Time *to return to newspaper work and to organize a daily paper of his own. The first issue of* PM *appeared in the middle of June, 1940, and the first major assignment Mr. Ingersoll gave himself as editor of the paper was to fly to London in October and report the Battle of Britain at first hand. The articles he wrote then appeared in* PM *and leading other newspapers throughout the country.* Report on England *reproduces them in somewhat expanded form.*